Overcoming:
Turning Trials into Triumphs

"What if our deepest wounds could become bridges to hope—
for ourselves and for others? In this deeply personal account,
Dr. DaSilva-Knapton reflects on some of life's most isolating
experiences, including infidelity, disability, and abuse. Honest
and insightful, Knapton's essays chart a path from hurt to
resilience, offering practical steps and hard-earned wisdom for
anyone seeking light in the darkness. From the particular details
of one life, a universal message emerges: you are not alone, and
we can overcome."
–Carleigh Beriont, PhD, educator, community organizer

Overcoming:
Turing Trials into Triumphs

By Lois DaSilva-Knapton

InsideOut Press
PO Box 2666
Country Club Hills, IL 60478

First edition April 2026

Cover design by Denise Daub
Interior design by Veronica Daub
Mountain images by Freepik

For more information about publishing services,
please visit www.InsideOutPress.com.

Printed in the United States of America

Library of Congress Control Number: 2026906821

ISBN-13: 979-8-9852054-9-7

To my grandchildren,

Victoria, Madyson and Xander:

Believe in your inner strength. Trust the light of your heart.
Grow with joy into the person you were meant to be, and face
each day with unshakable hope, unwavering kindness,
and endless possibility.

There are people who come into your life as students, and then there are the rare few who arrive as kindred spirits from the very beginning. Lois Knapton is one of those rare few for me.

I first met Lois in Derby, Connecticut, when I arrived to teach a Choice Theory® training at her school. I thought she was simply another participant in the room, eager to begin the process. What I didn't know was that Lois had already done years of work with Choice Theory before ever meeting me. In fact, she knew it so well, we moved her from the basic training into the advanced practicum where she belonged. Before long, she was certified and, later, became a basic instructor herself.

But what stands out most to me from those early days is not the training, but the connection. Our conversations flowed easily and deeply. Our values aligned. We began traveling to Choice Theory events together, laughing, learning, and talking endlessly about human behavior, emotional responsibility, and the power of choosing a better life—even in the face of incredible hardship. We truly became soul sisters along the way, realizing we both knew the pain of tragedy and trauma.

When Lois asked me to write the foreword to this book, I felt honored—not as an author or instructor, but as her friend. Lois is one of the most resilient, courageous, and authentically loving people I have ever known. Reading her story, even knowing some of it already, still moved me deeply.

Overcoming: Turning Trials into Triumphs is more than a recounting of difficult life experiences. It is a roadmap for reclaiming one's life with purpose, integrity, faith, and fierce determination. Lois writes with a raw honesty that disarms you, a wisdom earned through fire, and a compassion that reminds you that healing is always possible—no matter where you begin.

Her life is threaded with the principles at the heart of Choice Theory and Mental Freedom®, often long before she had the language for them. She instinctively chose responsibility over blame, truth over denial, courage over fear, and possibility over despair. Throughout this book, she demonstrates what it looks like to take control of one's thinking, reframe painful experiences, access inner resilience, and move forward one intentional choice at a time.

What astonishes me most is not what Lois survived, though she faced more adversity than many do in a lifetime, but who she became because of it. She turned suffering into strength, chaos into clarity, and tragedy into purpose. She chose to love her children fiercely, to rebuild her life piece by piece, and to pursue her own growth with humility and passion. Her story is not a story of victimhood; it is a testament to the extraordinary power of the human spirit when anchored in truth and supported by healthy relationships.

If you are holding this book because you are seeking hope, guidance, or courage, you could not be in better hands. Lois does not preach from a pedestal. She reaches back with empathy, honesty, and lived experience, offering the kind of guidance that only someone who has walked through the storm can give. Her strategies are practical. Her insights are profound. And her heart is wide open.

Lois truly embodies the spirit of an overcomer—not because she was free from hardship, but because she kept choosing her way through it. Each chapter invites you to discover that same strength within yourself.

It is my honor to stand beside her, both in our decades of Choice Theory work and in this beautiful offering to the world.

–Kim Olver, author of Mental Freedom, *Choice Theory instructor, coach, and friend*

Introduction

You are an overcomer. Believe it or not, you have the power, courage, and perseverance inside you to overcome any obstacle in your way. You simply need to have realistic goals and persistence.

This book is a compilation of many stories from my life; read it from cover to cover or bounce around. The names have changed, but the situations have not. Each chapter will start with a story from my life, and then we'll delve into specific strategies to overcome that situation.

I am writing this book to empower you to break through the barriers holding you back from being your best self, overcome obstacles amidst chaos and unknowns, and persevere against all odds. Stand up for your values and beliefs while not caring about what people think, be compassionate and empathetic along your courageous route, and don't trample people—bring them along if they want to join you on your journey.

Although I've been told I wear rose-colored glasses, I know everything is not peaches and cream. Behind those glasses lurk good work ethic, persistence, and obstinance. I persist through the obstacles stopping me from obtaining my goals, and I want to share this mindset with you. It can be challenging and slow-going, but you can overcome anything. I believe in you. You picked up this book today for a reason.

We all face adversity. How do we get through it? With perseverance, grit, faith, positivity, self-reflection, honesty, authenticity, passion, and drive.

I endured sexual abuse at the young age of three that went undetected until I was forty-two. My feelings of abandonment were predicated on my mother's first divorce from my biological father, who disappeared from my life. I was seven. She divorced six more times during my first thirty years of life. I suffered physical and emotional abuse at the hands of my father, some stepfathers, and my husband. I was encouraged to leave my husband only after I had turned to alcohol for comfort while he turned to infidelity. A severe heart condition threatened my existence—yet why did I push on? Some people shut down while others push through. Then my son died at just twenty-nine years old: a mother's worst nightmare. No parent should outlive their child.

I didn't know it then, but I was accessing Choice Theory. In the late '60s, William Glasser developed this theory to explain behavior. The premise is that we all strive to fulfill our needs, relationships are essential, and we are responsible for all our actions. Simple, right?

After realizing I was a thirty-five-year-old mother and waitress with no other skills, I started substitute teaching. My husband nagged, "Why don't you get a real job?" In his mind, teachers were not valued. I landed a job as an aide in a high school classroom, and during those years, the principal offered training in William Glasser's Choice Theory and Reality Therapy.

When I started thinking about my thinking, which is called metacognition, I realized that my thoughts were compelling—they were driving me. The ideas in my mind either gave me confidence or drained me. Desiring to control that, I dove into the concepts of Choice Theory. This training changed my life and assisted me in getting out of a failed marriage, raising children with love and affection as a single mother, and focusing on the importance of relationships. Now, I focus on finding joy amid chaos.

These anecdotes are just the tip of the iceberg. The book has many more details, each with encouraging strategies to apply to your obstacles.

OVERCOMING
Financial Difficulties

"Real wealth is not about money. Real wealth is about freedom"
–James Clear

I was a stay-at-home mom and a waitress. I was married, and we had three kids, a golden retriever named Samber, two cars, and a house with a mortgage—the picture-perfect family. My husband worked in sales. I was a part-time aerobic instructor and volunteer president of the parent teacher organization. My kids went to dance, gymnastics, karate, private preschool, and full-day kindergarten. Life was good until it was not. I thought I had it all until it all came crashing down.

After those carefree years in high school and college, all I did was trudge through the day attending to my husband, the family, the kids, the dog, the house—but my heart wasn't in it. It's funny, the things we think will fulfill our happiness. I searched for that magic bullet of joy, and for a long time—even during my dysfunctional twelve-year marriage—I thought we had it all. My husband had a reasonably good job. We had a roof over our heads and food in our bellies. Security is what life is about, right?

Deep in my core, I was not satisfied. I now know that I wanted genuine connection and unconditional love; I wanted to raise happy, healthy children. I wanted them to understand what a loving relationship looks like, but I realized that the relationship I was modeling for my children was not healthy.

It's easy to pretend when you're out in the real world, but when you go home and close your doors, all the pretending goes away, and we stand naked—our true selves are exposed. When I looked in the mirror, I did not like my true self. I was stuck in an abusive, unhealthy marriage, and I needed to find the strength and courage to get out. I realized my most significant barrier was finances. With no real training or job to fall back on, I did not believe I could be alone and provide for three children. The stay-at-home mom and waitress lifestyle truly never crossed my mind as a career choice. That career path would never provide medical insurance or pay the mortgage and school tuition.

So, on that final, fateful day, after more than a year of private counseling, preparatory activities, and stashing away specialty items in boxes, I told the kids to grab their backpacks and we jumped in the car. With great trepidation and fear, I drove away amid a screaming fight with my husband of twelve years. He never dreamed I would gather enough money to leave him. I was not sure either. I later learned that my new apartment complex was tagged "The Divorced Women's Complex." No wonder the rent was so cheap. I had squirreled away enough money and borrowed money from friends to pay for it. Money. It always comes down to money. How would I ever have enough money to survive?

The two-bedroom apartment was run-down and unfurnished, but upon opening the door, I realized I had done it. I broke free. As I stood there with three kids, three backpacks, and an empty apartment, the tears started flowing. How in the world can I do this? What on earth was I thinking? I did not have any family around that could assist me. My mother lived in Florida, and my siblings were scattered throughout the country. It seems everyone had run away. My negative self-talk started to get the best of me until my daughter tugged on my coat sleeve. She said, "Mommy, are we having a sleepover?" Proudly displaying her pajamas, her 9-year-old twin sister asked, "Where are the beds?" Thankfully, I had packed some blankets in the trunk of the car. We slept that night, snuggled together, on the floor of that new apartment using our backpacks as pillows. The following day, when we awoke, my 9-year-old daughter proudly pulled out four spoons from her backpack. "Mommy, I packed some spoons so we could have cereal for breakfast," she said. My heart sank. I didn't even have any cereal in the cabinet. I thanked God for the complimentary breakfast and lunch at school. My kids were going to need it.

I had already researched where the bus would pick up my kids and when the bus would arrive. After brushing our teeth, each child threw on the outfit they had packed in their backpack and went off to school. My son was in kindergarten, and the girls were in fourth grade then. We were ready to embark on the next adventure in our lives.

I went directly to the state offices to see what help I could get, and waiting in that long line of people, I looked around the room and thought to myself, *I don't belong there. I'm not like them.* Out-of-control kids roamed around the waiting area, screaming with tangled messes of hair and food crusted on their faces. A child approached me with her sticky lollipop hands, stepping over the junk food bags crumpled on the floor while her nineteen-year-old mother nursed her baby. Other babies were left buckled in their car seats on the floor while their parents smoked outside. Some of the parents looked beat up, literally beat up, with black eyes hiding behind sunglasses. Some parents looked high and others like they were on their last leg. On that day, I vowed that I would use the system as long as I needed it, but then I would get out of it.

After two and a half hours, I finally saw a worker in the waiting room. State workers are overworked and underpaid, and they talk like robots. The worker started her spiel, describing the services they could offer and the paperwork I needed to produce. Since my income was zero, I walked away with health insurance for my family, women's infant and children's supplemental food, and food stamps. They informed me about the food shelters, told me where there was one in my town, and set up an appointment to return to finish my paperwork. I remember crying all the way home. I was trying to figure out how to pay for electricity, food, and gas. How do you pay for something when you don't have any money? What do they expect me to do? Escaping my husband took me almost a year of saving to afford a security deposit on the shabby two-bedroom apartment I could secure.

The next step was to head to the grocery store with my newfound food stamps. Our new diet included macaroni and cheese, peanut butter and jelly, ramen noodles, and spaghetti. I cooked spaghetti in a frying pan stashed away in our camping gear, which I had squirreled away in the trunk of my car without notice. I had grabbed some plastic silverware from McDonald's that morning when I purchased my small cup of tea. I also grabbed a handful of salt, pepper, and sugar. I wondered if I was stealing, but then I decided it was out on the counter for the taking, and I was a customer. The paper plates were also from the camping gear stash. We sat on the floor that night, eating spaghetti and playing "I spy with my little eye." Day two arrived, and I felt a little sense of accomplishment, but I had to send the kids to school in the same clothes they wore the day before. I knew if I didn't get different clothes for the third day, I would get a call from the principal asking why the kids didn't have extra clothes. That day, when the kids were in school, I would sneak back into my old house and grab some of the boxes I had so neatly stashed away.

These were callous financial times for my children and me; no one was there to help me through that crisis. I had three children under my care and had to make it work. Slowly but surely, one step at a time, I continued to set goals. Next on the list is a better job. Waitressing was not going to pay the bills. Now that I was a single mother, I needed a job during the day when my kids were in school. I scoured the newspapers and read all the advertisements on the bulletin board at the grocery store. Finally, I saw an advertisement for a paraeducator at our local high school.

I had no experience in this position but applied for the job anyway. I took a leap of faith. I had to. While in the interview process, once again, my negative self-talk tried to take over: *Who am I joking? I've never worked in a school system before. Who's going to hire me without any experience?* As always, I held my head high and pretended I was confident. When asked the question, "What experience do you have?" I answered honestly,

"Zero. I have no experience working in a school system, but I have three children and am a quick learner." I recall the special education teacher saying, "I like her. Let's hire her".

I got that job. Back then in the late '90s, the starting pay as an aid in a school system was $6.25 an hour. My annual salary was $13,650. I was elated. I felt so proud to receive those paychecks, but that bubble burst as every penny of that paycheck was designated yet still not enough money to cover the rent and the electricity. Cable and cell phones were not luxuries we could afford. There were days when I was looking under the car mat for quarters just to put gas in my car so I could bring my kids to their sports outings. I always held my head high. Yeah, things were tough, things were callous. My kids didn't realize we were poor, but when they were older, they asked me, " We were pretty poor, weren't we?"

All I knew was I needed to use all the systems of support I could find and keep moving forward. I loved my kids dearly and wanted to show them that we can accomplish anything we want if we put our minds to it. I made friends with an auctioneer across the street from our housing complex. I volunteered for him, and he gave me a couch, beds, and dressers for our new apartment. I made everything into an adventure. It became fun. If you have ever sent your child off to college or set them up in a new apartment, you know what it takes to get set up. There are many things that ordinary people with regular incomes take for granted, such as a toilet brush, toilet plunger, toilet paper, paper towels, dish soap, hand soap, laundry detergent, and a washer and dryer. That's a whole other story. Taking my clothes back and forth to the laundromat was expensive. Sometimes, I couldn't afford to dry them, and I would bring them home wet, and we'd hang them all over the house. We treated it like a game, our tent of wet clothes. As the months went on, the weather got colder. The Divorced Women's Complex used electric heat, and that first winter, the electric bill came in at over $500. There was no way I could pay that bill. I called the company, and they said they couldn't help me. I just needed to pay the bill. I explained to them that I did not have the money to pay the bill. I asked to speak to the manager. Remember, never give up. If you can't conquer it, you can always go around it. After taking my complaint to the top of the ladder, I got on a payment plan. It took me eight more months to get out from under the electric bills from that winter. I agreed with the electric company and stuck to my word. Some programs will help defer or make payments, including energy assistance, if you qualify. Local churches might also help. That's how we can overcome. Lean on systems of support and set attainable goals to work out of those support systems.

The holidays were the worst. Just thinking about buying Halloween costumes for three kids was overwhelming, but Christmas was the most challenging. Recently, my daughter said to me as I wrapped a present for my 7-year-old granddaughter using paper bags, "You used to wrap all our presents in a newspaper, but at least you used the comics sections so they looked colorful." I choked up. I would take my kids to the recycling center to search through the newspapers for the comic strips. We used that paper to wrap presents if there were any to wrap. The first Christmas we spent on our own, I told the kids to look around their room and find a toy they could give to their sister or brother. That is how they spent Christmas, gifting their toys to each other. I spent many nights crying alone in my bedroom, but I never gave up.

The following Christmas, the school nurse came to me and whispered, "We want to help you. Can you tell me what size clothes your children will wear?" I burst into tears. I gave her the sizes for my twin ten-year-olds and my seven-year-old son. Thanks to her, Santa Claus arrived at my house. She gave me a large garbage bag full of presents, and my kids could not believe their eyes when they saw presents under the tree with real wrapping paper on them. To this day, I still have a gift that was given to me anonymously over twenty years ago by the school nurse. Someone labeled the present "to Mom from Santa." It was a necklace and a pair of earrings. Tears rolled down my face, and the kids said, "Mommy, who gave you that?" I told them, "Santa Claus. Santa Claus is real. Santa Claus is the spirit of giving, and the spirit of giving is mighty."

Now, I give as much as possible. I give to charities, sponsor children in Africa, and work in a helping profession. I often pay for the car behind me in the drive-through to "pay it forward." I love that surprised look on their face when the cashier tells them that the vehicle in front of them paid their bill. Try it sometime. It feels great!

Financial difficulties can be very overwhelming. If you find yourself in a challenging situation, it is crucial to take a step back and prioritize your needs. Of course, survival comes first: You need a roof over your head, food in your belly, clothes for your body, and shoes for your feet. Be sure to reach out and grab onto all the systems of care and support available to you during financially challenging times. Do not let your pride get in the way. Those systems are there for you to access when you need them. There are many services. You have to be willing to stand in many lines, fill out a lot of paperwork, and provide everything they are asking for. There are many hoops to jump through when you are accessing these support systems, but if you pay attention and do what they ask, you can make it through.

I continued my schooling, got a job during the school day, and bought a house on my own. My mom helped me with a $2,000 down payment for a home that was in foreclosure. I worked hard with the bank. The house cost $51,000. I remember signing that mortgage and thinking, *Wow, I did it; I bought a house alone.* I connected with the community support services to assist with fixing up the house, making it safe and energy efficient. Most communities have grant programs, energy assistance, and loan programs. You simply need to ask.

I participated in a thirteen-week program, Financial Peace University with Dave Ramsey, that helps people dump their debt, gain control of their money, and learn new financially responsible behaviors founded on commitment and accountability. The program reiterated that I could own my house with no mortgage if I focused. I could not envision owning a house outright without a mortgage. And guess what? Fifteen years later, I own two homes without a mortgage. It's unbelievable how dreams do come true if you maintain focus.

If you face financial challenges, prioritizing your needs is the first step. Assess where your money is truly going by writing down your incoming and outgoing cash flow. Create a clear budget and stick to it. That's what I did. You'd be surprised how much a coffee and a donut cost. I recently realized that my daily iced tea at $3.10 adds up. So, I stopped buying my daily iced tea and started making it at home. Every little thing you do with your finances matters. You have to decide if you can afford such luxuries.

Listing your needs separate from your wants is a vital step. Then, you can determine how much of your finances can go toward the luxuries you wish to have. When you stick to a budget, you continually assess your needs versus your wants, and every now and then, you can splurge on yourself. I do! It is essential.

Another financial tip is to transfer credit card debt to a short-term zero-percent credit card. Look for offers with your current credit cards and rotate the debt around. I called my creditors often. Someone told me that if you pay a creditor something, they cannot take you to court. So I called my creditor and said I wanted to give $5 a month. That's the best I can do. Even though the bill was for thousands of dollars, they said okay. Of course, they get to charge interest, which adds up, so be very careful about interest charges and pay attention to late fees.

Most importantly, do what you say and say what you mean. Stick to the plan. We can discuss financial ins and outs, strengths and weaknesses, and good and bad decisions, but pay attention to credit cards. It's best to not use them at all. Buying something with a credit card feels so good but paying it off takes so long. If you have a credit card, pay attention to the interest rate and ensure that your minimum payments pay all the monthly interest. Work with the people you owe bills to; they will work with you. But if you say you'll do something, you must follow through.

Remember, these bills only go away once you pay them or create a deal with the people you owe. Years ago, I found something online about student loan forgiveness. If I made ten years of on-time monthly payments—120 payments—on my student loans, I might get the rest of the loans forgiven. There are other stringent and specific criteria, too, but I applied anyway. Applying and getting accepted are two different things. I still owed more than $48,000, but I was delighted to think there might be a way out of this student loan debt.

After eighteen months, I received a final notice saying I had met all the criteria for loan forgiveness. After making ten years of monthly loan payments, I was being rewarded for it. You never know what it is on the other side of doing the next right thing.

According to student loan forgiveness statistics from educationdata.org, more students benefited from loan forgiveness in 2023, but the total amount forgiven was less than one percent of the national outstanding student loan debt balance. Only 2.3 percent of the Public Service Loan Forgiveness applicants have been accepted since November 2020, and I was one of them.

If you are in collections for over $10,000, contact the agency and ask how much they will allow you to pay off. They will usually cut it down by forty or fifty percent. Sometimes, you can secure a loan to pay it off at a lower interest rate. Sometimes, you can deal with credit bureau collection agencies or school loans in default. You would be surprised.

One last important thing to do about your finances is to run your credit report. The three major credit bureaus are Experian, Equifax, and TransUnion. These companies must provide you with one free copy of your credit report per year. Be careful because they are not required to provide your credit score; they often charge for that. CreditKarma.com or annaulcreditreport.com will also provide you with free credit reports. So run it, study it, and decide how to clean it up. Make sure you call these companies and get any strange charges off of your credit report. Your debt will never magically go away; it will haunt you for the rest of your life. Although after seven years, some old charges will drop off your credit report, you will still owe the debt. I have reiterated this to my kids over and over and over and over, "You need to pay your bills. It's the right thing to do." Only take the goods and services if you want the bills. It's a straightforward concept.

Years ago, I was talking to a friend, complaining, "I don't think

I'll ever have my house on the water." All my life, I have dreamed about living in a house on the water, any water—a lake, a river, or an ocean. I listened to my negative self-talk and started believing this would never happen. My friend said, "Why are you giving up on your dreams?" So, I changed my thoughts. I did not give up on my dreams. Today, I can walk out my front door and sit on the massive seawall by the ocean.

If you find yourself too deep into financial woes, the only way to get out is one step at a time, setting small goals, using the support systems around you, and believing you can do it. Like me, you are an overcomer. Nothing is impossible if you want it to happen. You can make it happen. You just have to want it bad enough.

Lessons Learned:

- Use all the systems of support you can find.
- Keep moving forward.
- If you put your mind to it, you can accomplish anything you want.
- Never give up.
- If you don't conquer it, you can always go around it.
- Set attainable goals to work your way out of support systems.
- Local churches can offer help.
- Santa Claus is real. Santa Claus is the spirit of giving, and the spirit of giving is mighty.
- Pay it forward.
- Take a step back and prioritize your needs.
- Have a very clear budget, and stick to it.
- If you are diligent and pay attention, you can make it through.
- Prioritizing your needs is the first step.
- Take a close look at the interest rates and the monthly fees for bank accounts.
- Do what you say and say what you mean.
- Bills only go away once you pay them.
- You never know what it is on the other side of doing the next right thing.
- Review your credit report.
- Your debt will never magically go away.
- Set small goals, use the systems of support that are around you.

Overcoming the
Loss of a Job

"If you always do what you've always done, you will always get what you always got." –often attributed to Henry Ford

It is 2020, and here I sit—unemployed but alive. I am certainly not alone, but it sure does feel like it. Losing your job is like losing your self-worth. It feels like everything I worked for has gone down the drain.

Along with the mental anguish comes financial instability—a combination that leads people to the dark side. I have been working all my life, and I never lost a job until I was fifty-seven years old. I am amazed at how those of us who are working take it for granted.

For me, each job change was a step up the ladder. I started working in my mom's retail store when I was fifteen. In my senior year in high school, I became a waitress, a job I kept for many years even after I became a mother. After my divorce, my goal was to get a different job, and as a single mother, I decided to pursue a job in education. I saw the call for the high school classroom aide position in the newspaper. With no relevant experience, I walked into that interview beaming with confidence. I repeatedly told myself, *You got this, you got this*. I landed that job and never looked back. At thirty-five years old, I was starting at the bottom rung of the career ladder, making $13,000 annually and living paycheck to paycheck. I continued my college courses while spending the week working as an aide and waitressing over the weekend.

By age forty, I was an administrator in a central office. At forty-one years old, I received my Doctoral Degree in Educational Leadership the same year my daughters graduated from high school. Throughout my educational career, I worked toward reaching my perceived pinnacle: school superintendent. I achieved this by age fifty-one. I changed the lives of thousands of children until I didn't. Ultimately, I was caught up in a political firestorm and burned. As always, I looked for the lesson in the muck. Getting burned helped me realize I needed a different job, but what could I do?

Moments like these are when you must stretch, believe in yourself, and examine your skills. We are always stuck in a Catch-22 when we've never done something, but we must do that something to go to the next level: If we don't have any experience in that arena, then we cannot improve. This cycle prevents us from moving in different directions. It takes courage to believe you can do something you've never done—but kids do this every day. When learning to ride a bike, they do not know how to ride the bike. They thrive when someone else believes in them, teaches them, and guides them. Alongside a mentor who assesses their developing skills, their ability to become more independent at riding that bike shines through.

We are all continually learning. The most important thing to remember is that you are worth it. You can do great things. With the proper support and the right mindset, you can overcome the obstacles before you. Courageous conversations with yourself are the key to moving forward, but you must have genuine faith that you will overcome. When doubt creeps in, it squashes your positive mindset. Push that doubt from your mind and start believing you can accomplish the task ahead of you.

Your thoughts matter. We have anywhere from 12,000 to 50,000 thoughts a day. According to the National Science Foundation, "Eighty percent are negative, and ninety-five percent are the same repetitive thoughts as the day before." Wouldn't it be nice to harness those thoughts and decide which ones to keep and which to let go? We can acknowledge them and choose which ones will benefit us and which ones will not benefit us: Dismiss those that don't, meditate on those that do, and be sure to set attainable goals.

It is up to us to stretch ourselves to reach new heights. Everything will always stay the same if we keep doing the same thing we have always done. I believed I could do the job, and it worked.

We all have bills. When I was working, I set up payments for direct deposit, and all the bills got paid. Now and then, I would have to dip into the overdraft account, but I could replace it on the next payday. It never crossed my mind that, someday, something might happen, and I would lose that job. During the pandemic, unemployment became the new normal, and millions of people lost their jobs—a scary reality.

Losing your job means going without what you are used to having, which often leads to a wide range of debilitating emotions: anger, despair, frustration, melancholy, and more. They will swallow us up if we allow ourselves to wallow in or act on these emotions. In these moments, it's important to think about your relationships—especially the one you have with yourself.

The late William Glasser tells us there are three ways to navigate relationships. The first way is to do nothing. In an ineffective relationship, I can still choose to do nothing because I prefer to keep the benefits I receive from that relationship. The second choice is to try to change the relationship, which requires both parties' willingness and effort. The third option is to leave the relationship. Keeping these three choices on the front burner has helped me tremendously. There's a saying that people come into your life for a reason or a season. Each person who touched my life was there to teach me something. Ultimately, I get to choose whether I stay or not.

These choices might sound selfish, but I can only control myself—an understanding that offers a lot of power. With this power comes the notion that I am responsible for my behavior. If I behave in a way that damages a relationship, I get to consider if I can or want to do something differently. Suppose I don't want to change my behavior and want to keep doing what I'm doing. The question becomes, "How much effort do I want to spend to make this work?" I can ask myself the same question. If I am wallowing in my jobless mindset and feeling less than others, I ask myself, "How hard do I want to work to change things?" It is ultimately up to me. No one and nothing can make me do anything. Only I can control what I do and how I feel.

I must create sanity by developing a mental guide for the disastrous moments in my life. Amid my most challenging professional experience of getting politically pushed out of a superintendent's position, I arrived at some lessons.

During a counseling session I had attended as one of my action steps during this challenging life transition, I recall my counselor declaring, "There is far more right with you than there is wrong with you." I finally believed it.

At my last superintendent meeting, a colleague stated, "We are watching people's careers ruined by dysfunctional boards and toxic communities." When the superintendent must turn their attention away from the kids and over to the demands of a small group of loud parents and politicians, the children ultimately get hurt. I was standing up for what I believed in, and it was not easy. My emotions were running very high; I thought everyone hated me. Was my perception really true?

The work of Byron Katie instructs us to ask:

1. Is it true? (If no, move to question three.)

2. Can you absolutely know that it's true?

3. How do you react when you believe that thought?

4. Who or what would you be without the thought?

These four questions have helped me many times in my life. Everyone comes from a different point of view, and everyone's perceptions are true only for them, so how can we know something is absolutely true? As a leader, it is essential to remember this. Our thoughts, values, and beliefs matter; they come from our upbringing and the lessons we've learned. When I think, *They hate me*, who exactly is "they," and how many are there? How can I know this is really true? Likely, I can't. I can change my thoughts. I can take other action steps. I can be in control of how I feel.

In my last job, I was their leader. I believed they should appreciate me for all my hard work, but they only criticized me, downgraded my ideas, and argued with my brainstorms. But similarly, they had their perceptions. I didn't understand how they could differ drastically from mine. Then came a hard realization: If people perceive something about me, I own a piece of that. My communication lands on people in a certain way. I have my way of being, and not everyone agrees with it. That is okay; I must be true to myself to keep myself balanced. I get to decide whether I want to make peace or not.

I was faced with a choice: Should I do nothing, something, or leave? Ignoring a hostile environment is an action step, but it rarely solves the problem. So, did they push me out? Is it all their fault? Self-evaluation is critical, and I couldn't agree with their point of view. In addition, there must be agreed-upon conditions of quality that we all measure ourselves by. Do we have a nurturing environment? Are we all giving our best effort? It is essential to define quality before the self-evaluation process occurs. Otherwise, your self-evaluation will be meaningless. For instance, I could say, "I'm doing a great job," and others can respond, "No, you're not," and there's no movement. I'm doing a great job based on what? The condition that determines the quality of that situation is the yardstick—and we need a yardstick. If we don't have a form of measurement, we will go through life as if everything is always fine.

The conditions of quality in a relationship are critical to understanding. We have different types of relationships: family, friends, colleagues, and authorities, for example. We behave in different ways based on the conditions of that relationship. A working relationship is very different from a relationship at home. My relationship with my husband and children differs significantly from that with my friends or authorities.

During my seven months without a job, I second-guessed myself, rehashing the events and wondering if I could have done anything differently. Ultimately, after all that time and all that thinking, I would do the same thing again. I would resign if the circumstances were the same. I often tell my children to take the next right step. That means something different for everyone. Wherever you are, stop, take a breath, and plan to do the next right thing to move you toward your goal.

I like to take my brother, Stanley's advice: Get on your knees to pray, then get on your feet and work. We cannot sit around and expect things to be different; we must do our part. As a very faithful person, I'd like to reiterate a famous story:

A man stood on his rooftop in a flood, praying to God for help. A rowboat came by a motorboat and a helicopter. Each time, the man said, "No, it's okay. I'm praying to God; he is going to save me." When the man eventually drowned, he went to heaven and told God, "I had faith in you, but you didn't save me!" God replied, "I sent you a rowboat, a motorboat, and a helicopter. What more did you expect?"

So, though I was without a job, I knew I had faith, but I also knew that I had to act. We cannot sit around and expect change without taking action steps. A job would not magically drop out of the sky into my lap. I cannot sit on my couch and say, "Oh, I am faithful that the Lord will provide." The Lord will provide, but we must do our part.

So, I sent out more than thirty applications. I also looked at a wide variety of jobs, including jobs that were a lower level than my last job, as well as jobs that were out of my league. I understood I might have to step down and do something different, maybe even go back to waitressing. All I knew was that I needed to take action, and I did. I remained faithful and did not let those negative emotions swallow me up.

There were some down days, but the good ones outweighed the bad. It was all a matter of perspective. My commute, which I took for six years, was twenty-three minutes through rural landscapes and winding back roads. I took that for granted, along with those direct deposit checks into my account every two weeks. I should have had a deeper level of gratitude for what I had.

Looking back on it now, I search for the GLOW: gifts, lessons, opportunities, and wisdom—a phrase coined by my good friend, nationally renowned author, speaker, and behavior expert, Kim Olver.

What gifts did I receive from unemployment? I developed a much deeper relationship with my husband, children, and grandchildren. I was around so much that my time felt unlimited. What lessons did I learn from this experience? I realized that I was stronger than I thought. I recognized that I must focus on genuine gratitude and appreciation daily. I learned that relationships could grow from the depths of despair.

So, it's true: Losing a job can have benefits, but I had to search for those benefits—much like people tried to find benefits of the pandemic. Some of those benefits included the ability to spend more time with those that we love, as many people connected with their children, spouses, parents, and grandparents in ways that they hadn't for years. They deepened their relationships. Unemployment taught people how to cut corners and what is truly important to them. The point is, do you need it, or do you want it? What steps do you take to protect the things that are most important to you? If you don't have food, where can you get it? There are places where you can get food. There are friends that you can depend on. It takes a keen understanding of who you are and where to find help when you need it. No matter what, it is scary. It is scary to do without. It is scary to think about the next day and wonder if your car will be repossessed or if your house will go into foreclosure.

Finally, I realized our mistakes don't limit us; only our fears do. As Maya Angelou said, "Hope and fear cannot occupy the same space; invite one to stay."

So, look at where you are now. What are your thoughts? What are you saying to yourself daily? What are you doing daily? What are your actions? What next step can you take toward doing the next right thing? Do you know where you're headed? What is your goal?

You can only get there if you know where you're headed.

Lessons Learned:

- Courageous conversations with yourself are the key to forward movement.

- Start believing that you truly can accomplish the task ahead of you.

- It is up to us to stretch ourselves to reach new heights.

- I am responsible for my behavior.

- There is far more right with me than is wrong with me.

- If people perceive something about me, I own a piece of that.

- Wherever you are right now, just stop, take a breath, and plan to do the next right thing.

- Hold tight to a deeper level of gratitude for what you have.

- Our mistakes don't limit us; only our fears do.

OVERCOMING
Physical Abuse

"Pain is inevitable. But suffering is optional." –Haruki Murakami

I wondered if this would be the end of my life—right there, in my own house, by my husband's hands. I was able to get free and run for the phone. It was long enough ago that the phone was attached to the wall and had a long cord, a handle, and a rotary dialing system. I grabbed the phone handle and put my finger in the nine on the rotary dial, pulling that circle to the top, and listening as the dial slowly ticked backward. *Tick, tick, tick.* I did not know if I would have time to dial 9-1-1. He came around the corner and grabbed my neck. I'll never forget the words he said: "I could kill you before they get here." With one hand wrapped around my neck, his other hand simultaneously ripped the phone off the wall. I tried to stare him down, but tears just rolled down my cheeks. He released the choke hold in silence, and I dropped to the floor, dizzy and dazed. I held tightly to the phone handle as I realized the other end was no longer attached to anything. My message to the world would go nowhere. I would continue to live within these four walls of dysfunction in my house, with my three-year-old son and six-year-old twin girls. The front door remained closed, harboring the secret of deep despair. Nobody would believe this was truly happening to me and my family. How did it ever begin? How did it ever get this far? How could I ever escape to safety? He constantly told me he would kill me if I tried to leave, and I believed him.

We were high school sweethearts, and I honestly thought I

had met the love of my life, although my sister didn't think so. She thought he was a big, arrogant jerk and would ask me why he was always so angry. I didn't see it then. It's funny how we don't see the signs when we don't want to see them—strange how we can artfully rationalize our way through anything. Even though the old 1963 Dodge Dart windshield had been broken at least three times by him, he always had an excellent reason why he broke it. Usually, it was because I "made" him so mad. Back then, I believed it.

Now I know better. No one *makes* anyone feel or do anything. We all control ourselves and no one else. Eric slammed the rearview mirror so hard against the windshield in a rage. I always sat silently in the passenger seat, pretending I wasn't there, trying to make it all better, but nothing I did was right. I couldn't even breathe correctly for him. During those fits of rage, I would try to breathe quietly to prevent upsetting him more. As I write this now, I can't believe I was so submissive, blaming myself for his regressions and believing I must have pushed him to it, which is what he always told me. It was always my fault. What a crazy thing, making sure I breathe quietly to avoid disturbing my raging boyfriend—my future husband.

I did not have any examples of healthy, loving relationships in my life, so I thought it was normal; I didn't know any better. My mom, with her multiple divorces, wasn't a great role model. I just thought relationships came and went. During another rage in that old Dodge Dart, I remember thinking he might rip the steering wheel off the car as I watched him hold it tightly, shaking and yanking in his rage. I thought it was okay and that this anger would all go away after we got married. What a silly thing to believe.

Little did I know that this cycle of abuse would become my lifestyle. It works like a circle. The abuse comes in waves and builds up at the top of the circle. The abuse lasts for a period of time—could be days, weeks, months, or longer—before the explosion occurs at the bottom of the circle. Then comes the guilty plea, which typically includes phrases like, "I love you. I need you. You mean the world to me. I'm so sorry. I'll never do it again. Let's make it work." Fantastic make-up sex usually concluded the cycle—lovemaking so genuine and honest that it makes me feel my abuser truly believes, at that point, that they are loving.

But then, when I least expect it, the cycle starts over again. I can't even tell you the catalyst for any of these fits of rage. I only remember the devastating outcome of the broken glass all over the floor when Eric swept the kitchen table clean with his arm. I always told the kids that their daddy was behaving badly and that they needed to go to their rooms. For years, the physical abuse was only against objects, not people. I had to think of a way to keep the children safe, and over time, it became customary for them. When they heard Daddy get upset, I didn't have to tell them to run to their room; they knew to go to their room and close their door. Thankfully, he rarely went into the bedrooms to chase the children. I used to rationalize that the abuse wasn't that bad. When it did get physical, it only entailed shoving and pushing, not punching—and he never touched the children, just me—so it couldn't be that bad, right?

Shoving. That's how it began a long time ago. We had graduated from high school, I had gone to college, and Eric had gone off to the military. A year and a half later, I was quitting college, getting his car from his parents, and driving eighteen hours to live with Eric on the military base. We were married soon after. The military lifestyle felt both freeing and prison-like at the same time. Everything seemed okay. We had our place in a trailer park with our dog; I was re-enrolled in a different college and commuting while Eric was training for his military career. Drug testing was standard in the military, but alcohol was allowed, so alcohol was the outlet. And there was a lot of alcohol.

One night in my early twenties, I went to the bar with some girlfriends while my husband was out of state on military training. As we were leaving, a fight broke out in the parking lot, and I found myself smack dab in the middle of the crowd that surrounded the brawl. Watching the fight, standing shoulder to shoulder with drunk strangers, was surreal. People had picked sides and were shouting. I was already scared before I saw someone throw down a knife. At the sound of sirens approaching, the crowd quickly dispersed. One of the drunken brawlers threw a knife on the ground; it had a beautiful white marble handle and a gleaming blade. I watched it skid under a car, and for a fleeting moment, I thought the knife was stunning—then one of my friends shouted, "Run!" So I did, leaving the knife behind.

As I reflected on the fight the next day, I remembered that knife and returned to the parking lot to search for it. There it was, underneath that same car. I brought it home and put it in a safe place. Deep down, I thought I might need that knife someday. That incident was almost thirty-five years ago, and I still have that knife somewhere.

Time went on, and I got pregnant. At five months, I discovered I was pregnant with twins. I was completing my senior year of college. It was both exciting and challenging. The twins were born, I graduated from college, and we moved out of that tiny trailer into a two-bedroom duplex thanks to military housing. We were moving up in the world. One day, both babies were crying. As a twenty-three-year-old first-time mother with twin infants, living on a military base without any family around, I felt so isolated. It was very challenging to deal with two crying infants simultaneously. I was cradling one of the infant twins in my arms when I noticed Eric's rage start to boil, and suddenly, he grabbed my shoulders and slammed me against the wall.

Everything went into slow motion. I was back in my childhood, playing the egg-toss game, where you toss an egg back and forth and try not to break it. You have to catch it gently to make sure it doesn't break on impact. I remember thinking my baby was like that egg. I slid down the wall and landed on my butt, the baby still in my arms.

Experience taught me that nothing I could do would change the situation, so I had moved into a pattern of silent obedience. The baby was still crying, but she was safe. I wanted to scream, but I sat very still and quiet as tears dripped down my cheeks. How could I raise my children in this household?

I was taken back to my father, in line beside my young siblings: *As the belt swings in the air, I stand frozen—silent and ready for the blow*. As far back as I can remember, I was a happy, playful child, even amid physical abuse. At the tender age of five, all seven siblings were lined up in the common area when Dad came home from work. We were required to stand side-by-side, shoulder to shoulder, while siblings were called out for misbehaving. I was the middle child. "Which one of you was bad today?" my father boomed. As soon as one confessed, we each got the belt. Silently standing in line while waiting my turn, I always tried to be brave, but in the end, tears ensued. I still wonder how a mother could watch her children being hit over and over again. Even as an adult, when I see a man unbuckle their belt and yank it out of their waistband, the sudden fear still encompasses me.

In my newfound motherhood, I vowed to never allow anyone to lay a hand on my children. I was very optimistic; I truly believed our marriage could improve. I was so excited during the happy days of the abuse cycle. Once, there was a time when we went two months without a fit of rage. I thought I was in heaven, but the cycle always continued eventually, and the years stretched on.

Finally, I went to counseling when my kids were five and eight. I even went to a battered women's shelter one night for safety. I saw other women with black eyes and casts on their arms and legs. Once again, I rationalized that my situation wasn't that bad. It was just a few strangleholds, some pushing and shoving, lots of yelling, and many broken dishes. One day, that all changed when I found charges for dinner and a bottle of wine on the credit card bill. I had suspected it for years, and now, I finally had evidence that my husband was cheating on me. I got the nerve to confront him when he came home from a DJ gig. As always, alcohol was involved, and the conversation did not go well. He ended up punching me. He wanted the punch to land in my stomach, but I turned just as the punch slammed into my hip bone. For me, that was the last straw. A few days later, I had an appointment with my gynecologist, and she saw the four-inch black-and-blue bruise on my hip. She looked at me and asked, "Are you in trouble?" My silence shattered as I broke down, finally telling someone what was really going on in my life.

I finally started to develop a plan to leave for good. I bought a book called *Getting Free: You Can End Abuse and Take Back Your Life* by Ginny NiCarthy, MSW. I covered that book with a brown paper bag so nobody would see the title when I read it. I kept the book hidden, but I read it often and learned many tricks about leaving an abusive relationship. The author explained the importance of maintaining a getaway bag with clothing and essentials for myself and my children in case we needed to make a quick escape. Following the book's advice, I kept a spare key to the car and the house hidden in a safe place, and I began secretly stashing as much money as possible for when I finally got out. I started packing boxes of the most precious items I wanted to take when the time came and kept them hidden up in the attic.

During one of those calm periods within the cycle of abuse, we both decided to go to independent counselors to save our marriage. I was hopeful this might work. After about seven weeks of independent sessions, I asked my therapist if we could do couples therapy, and she said she'd reach out to Eric's therapist to get the ball rolling.

One Saturday night, as I have done so many other Saturday nights, I threw on my apron and went to wait tables at the fine dining restaurant where I worked for seven years. As I was plating the food to bring out to my customers, the hostess told me I got a call and needed to get to the phone immediately. Expecting the babysitter, I was shocked to hear my therapist sounding stern and frantic. She had spoken to my husband's therapist, and she now feared for my life. I stood there in the restaurant lobby, wondering what in the world she was getting at. In a state of denial, I felt frustrated about being pulled from work, worried that my customer's food was getting cold. "Do you have any guns in the house, and do you know where the ammunition is? Has your husband ever talked about suicide?" she asked. I was dumbfounded. She told me not to go home, leave work immediately, and drive directly to the women's shelter—but my kids were at home with the babysitter.

As always, my self-talk got in the way—the constant stream of rationalizations. *I can fix this. I can make it all better. He will change. Just wait and see. Just love him a little more.* As I reflect on them, I can't understand how I was able to rationalize it all away, but I understand why: I wanted so badly for the relationship to work, I wanted to experience my fiftieth wedding anniversary with my loving husband, and I did not want to get divorced. The Bible had pounded into my psyche that divorce is wrong, and you can only get divorced under certain circumstances. *Was this circumstance enough?*

I thanked the therapist for her due diligence, hung up the phone, and continued working until my shift was over. Then I drove home because it was the only place I had to go. My husband's car was in the driveway when I arrived. The kids were sound asleep, and the house was eerily quiet. Something was not right. Feeling uneasy, I slowly opened the bedroom door.

My husband sat on the edge of the bed, staring blankly, seemingly in a trance. The butt of a shotgun was planted solidly between his feet, with the other end wedged under his chin. As I looked on the image that is seared in my memory forever, I recalled the day my husband taught me how to shoot with that gun. Today was different. Beer bottles, like shotgun shells, were scattered all over the floor. I closed the door, sat on the living room couch, and waited silently. We never spoke of the incident.

Soon after, I was finally brave enough to speak truthfully to my counselor, just sputtering on about my real-life issues as if discussing Sunday brunch. When I finally looked over, her face was sullen—mouth agape. I asked why she looked so shocked. She took a deep breath and said, "Don't you see? You're in the middle of a minefield." No, I didn't see that, no matter how careful I was, every step I took would be an explosion. As the realization sank in, I knew I had to get myself and my children out of that minefield without getting blown up.

Knowing I could get out, my spirits lifted a little more each day, and I became stronger. But there was a lot of work ahead of me, and I was scared. My negative self-talk often brought me down. *Can I do this alone with three children? I'm just a waitress.* I had yet to learn how I would support them, but time went on, and I continued stashing money away, packing boxes, and acting like the good wife my husband wanted me to be. Little did I know that he was snooping around my things.

One day, I was leaving the step aerobics class I taught at the town hall, which had a daycare, when I heard screeching tires. I looked up to find my husband in his Ford pickup, stopped in the middle of the main street, in a rage. I froze with my three kids tucked behind me. He was flailing that book, *Getting Free*, screaming, "What is this shit? Who are you getting free from, me? Yeah, you think so, right? You'll never be free." As he tore at the book, I watched the wind gently whisk the pages away, standing still as I quietly waited for him to finish his raging. It took a lot of strength not to run into the middle of the road, pound my fists on his chest and face, and beat him raw. Instead, I stood firmly in my spot, holding my children's little shaking hands. I tried to appear solid and confident on the outside, even as I shook like a leaf on the inside. He continued to scream at the top of his lungs, "Get over here right now and get in this truck!"

Bystanders stopped to watch the erratic scene. Some people began gathering up the pages of the book. The children were crying and cowering behind me. I had to make a decision. I waited for him to finish like I always did. I knew he would eventually realize what he was doing and how many people were watching him. This public display was validating, but I also felt exposed. Now the whole town knew we weren't the perfect family down the street, a loving couple with three kids and a golden retriever. Finally, he left the scene in a huff, and I calmed the children, put them in the car, and drove home. At that time, it was the only place I had to go, but I vowed to continue my plan to get out. However, no matter how optimistic I was, a piece of me always thought his words would come true: "If you leave, I will find you and kill you. I need you. You can't leave me." I continued taking that book's advice. Despite the doubt, I kept believing I would get out—I would get us all out safely.

If you are experiencing anything like this, know that it doesn't have to be this way. We always have three choices when we face problems in relationships: do nothing, try to change it, or leave. I became much stronger when I realized it was within my power to escape. I remember the deep shame and guilt I felt when I told my story for the first time. I didn't want anyone to know that this could happen to me. I was a strong-willed, independent woman on the path to success. How could this man have this much control over me? Our self-talk is so powerful; that shame and guilt held me back for so long. When I finally realized what I truly wanted and what I could achieve, my children were ages six, nine, and nine. I did get out safely, and I never looked back.

Lessons Learned:

- No one *makes* anyone do anything.

- We all control ourselves and no one else.

- Abuse is a cycle, like a circle.

- Rationalizing doesn't change your situation.

- Shatter your silence and tell the truth about your experience.

- Don't allow negative self-talk to bring you down.

- Believe you can and will get out.

- We always have three choices when facing problems in our relationships: do nothing, try to change it, or leave.

- Self-talk is powerful.

OVERCOMING
Child Sexual Abuse

"Sometimes, the emotions we are feeling belong to the person we are in a connection with, and an energetic cord must be severed." –Daily OM

When I was forty-five, I finally started digging into my recovery, seeking out therapists, rebirthing experiences, meditation, and Yoga. Through all these healing experiences, I still felt as if I was missing something in my life. I felt unable to love another person romantically. I felt lost and distant in my broken marriage, as if a cement wall was surrounding my heart.

I started seeing a Reiki therapist for healing sessions. The sessions were meditative and non-suggestive, like getting a massage for your mind. We met once a week for nearly eight months, and it was the best thing I ever did for myself. Even though I wasn't sure if I was getting anywhere, I knew I always enjoyed that hour of quiet meditation and energy healing. It was during one of these sessions that the unthinkable breakthrough occurred. I have heard of people not remembering traumatic events for many years, but I never understood how, when a traumatic event occurs, we can block it out of our memory until we are ready to heal.

The vision appeared, clear as can be: A family member and his friend, both of them thirteen-year-old boys, and me, just three years old at that time, being held as they explored my privates with their fingers. The abuse revealed itself to me forty-two years later, exploding like a volcano. I let out a shrill wail, catching the healer off guard. I did not know what to do with this information, nor did she. I did not tell another soul.

I was always a very bubbly, joyful child, always laughing, giggling, and singing—and like most kids, I wanted to please the older people in my life. Everybody called me Little Loey, and I was loved. I did not worry about the world. It didn't bother me that everybody else got more attention than me, a middle child with four older and two younger siblings, because I just went my merry way. I still wonder why that family member, Frank, picked me and not one of my older or younger siblings.

This new information was so clear, but I wondered, could I have made it up? How could I have not remembered this over all these years? Our brains can suppress traumatic events, but our cells remember the trauma. Alone, I started to process this new information. Weeks and months went by, and I buried the news again. I had a secret I was keeping from myself, but now it was out in the open, and I didn't know who to tell. I looked at toddlers in the grocery store in a different light, imagining a monster doing something—something that toddlers couldn't understand—and then telling those innocent children to keep it a secret.

At this point in my life, my kids were in their twenties. I recalled back when my twins were thirteen months old, I took them to a babysitter, Alison, who had been doing in-home care for one of my colleagues for many years. She had a daughter of her own and only liked babysitting girls, claiming boys were too challenging to handle. I thought I had vetted my babysitter, but I was unaware that her husband was usually at home, on disability from a back injury. His name was Bear. A few weeks after taking my twins to this babysitter, I was changing one of their diapers when she said, "Bear hurt," and pointed to her privates. I immediately drove to my babysitter's house, gathered everything that belonged to me and my children, and said we would never return. I did not speak with Alison about the incident. I did take my girls to the doctor, who found a minor swelling and redness around the vaginal area but no other evidence of abuse. I was devastated. How twisted does someone have to be to fondle an infant? I felt sick to my stomach, guilty and ashamed. Telling my husband was another story. It took all my power to keep him from going to that babysitter's house with a gun.

By the time my son was five and the girls were eight, we found a new babysitter, Diane. I never had a problem with her, and my children seemed to love her. She babysat every Saturday night for three years. Those nights, my husband would DJ, and I would waitress. Many years later, when my children were in their twenties, we saw Diane at the mall. I said, "Let's go say hello," and the girls refused. I found this very strange, and neither of them wanted to explain. I continued, "Why wouldn't you want to say hi? We could show her what great people you grew up to be." Their reactions did not change. I couldn't understand why my adult children were saying "no" so emphatically. I glanced over across the mall and caught Diane's eye, but continued on, my heart sinking. It was a bizarre moment. It was then that I realized there must be something I didn't know.

Driving home, just like when my children were little, I used the car ride as a discussion venue and asked why they didn't want to greet their old babysitter. That's when I learned that Diane would ask the girls to kiss her on the cheek, touch her breasts, and give her massages. Thankfully, clothes always stayed on, but sexual abuse is sexual abuse—a bad touch is a bad touch—no matter what.

Years later, my daughter told me she found Diane on social media and sent her a message: "You are a mother now? I hope your kids never have to deal with you touching them like you touched me and my sister. What you did to us was unacceptable. How can you even live with that? You are sick. I hope you got some help because being a mother isn't easy, and you surely can't raise healthy kids with your predatory mindset." Writing this message was cathartic for my daughter and aided her in her healing.

If you've ever experienced a bad touch, I am genuinely sorry. When it comes to getting over child sexual abuse, there is no easy path. Acknowledging that it occurred is the first step; understanding and accepting that it's not your fault is the key to overcoming the situation.

After gaining this information about my own bad-touch

experience, I questioned myself for two years. I wondered if I was too happy a child—if I was too gullible, too naive. I wondered if I had done something wrong. I wondered if it was supposed to be a punishment from God, if I wore too many skirts without shorts underneath, or if I smiled too much. I wondered if my mother knew. I wondered if Frank ever did this to anyone else. Why did Frank pick me? Why didn't I say anything? As a three-year-old, I was incapable of considering any of these questions. As a forty-five-year-old, these thoughts taunted me.

After a couple of years of processing this information alone, I decided to share it with my mother, but first, I wanted to be clear in my mind what my expectations were for sharing this information—but I didn't know what I expected. I just wanted to share this information with her. I wanted someone else to know, and I figured my mother was the right choice. Although I wasn't expecting anything from her, I was baffled and hurt when she gave me nothing—no reaction, no conversation, no questions— just a silent nod. I asked my mom to keep it to herself, explaining that I was embarrassed and didn't want to cause any waves in the family, and she said she would. So, I went on with my life as I always had, still trying to digest and heal from the incident.

Someone once told me that if you want to keep something a secret, do not tell anyone. I was reminded of this advice when, a few months after telling my mother, the information circled back to Frank. I was livid about the betrayal. Even though I know who my mother is, I thought this time would be different, considering that I was an adult who told her one of the worst things a child could go through in confidence, but my mother has always had difficulty thinking about others. She loves to stir things up, and I suspect that this gossip was just too juicy to stay sealed. She needed to open that can of worms. Unfortunately, it was buried in the dirt, swallowed up by the worms, unable to surface and reveal the truth.

I was almost fifty and had harbored this truth for over five years; the perpetrator had been hiding this truth for decades. My sister reminded me about a years-old court case involving Frank and the sexual abuse of his child; I had completely forgotten about it. He was never convicted and still claims his innocence. When I eventually did speak with Frank, I was not expecting an apology. However, I also was not expecting the severe denial from him, but I did not push the issue. What for? Everyone always sticks to their story. We never spoke about it again. However, I finally broached it with my counselor in recent years. I have finally put that trauma to rest for good, and forgiveness has freed me. But many children are not free.

In my current career as an educational administrator, I have attended multiple trainings on sexual abuse and trafficking, which is a big business where people make large sums of money. It turns my stomach to think that other people would abuse children in sexual ways for monetary gain. I thank God that my encounter with sexual abuse was short-lived—one incident at the bottom of the attic stairs, even though it is forever seared in my memory.

As I continue my work in the educational system, I keep my eyes open for any child showing signs of withdrawal, denial, or unexplained defensiveness. I'm a mandated reporter, so if I see anything unusual, I must report the incident. The pandemic made this difficult. Because school was held remotely due to COVID-19 restrictions, it did not allow school staff to lay eyes on the children as often as we would like. Remote learning from spring 2020 through fall 2021 only worsened conditions for our most vulnerable children as they were kept in their homes. It was a very trying time for our nation, a time that will require years to heal educationally, socially, and mentally.

An overcomer is always moving forward. I continue to reflect and move forward as an adult with my bad-touch experience. Healing from child sexual abuse takes time, understanding, and forgiveness. The forgiveness is for me, not the perpetrator. The process of forgiveness and releasing thoughts and feelings that have kept you tied to the past can occur without the other person's participation. It brings freedom from shame and guilt that keeps us in the prison of the past.

I heard the saying once, "If you continually look in the rearview mirror, you can't see where you are going." As a visual person, I really enjoy that saying. The late William Glasser also reminded us that the past is the past; we can process the past in the present without dwelling on the past. For example, I can process my feelings today as a sixty-year-old woman regarding the incident when I was three or my parents' divorce when I was seven. Then, process my current feelings around that situation. Instead of dwelling on the facts of the past, I consider my present feelings, thoughts, and actions so I can develop plans to move forward.

Overcomers have goals. Overcomers make plans. Overcomers do not dwell on the past. Overcomers do not become the victims. Overcomers do not play the proverbial violin. Overcomers do not say, "Poor me, poor me! Everything was awful for me, and I'm never going to get any better." Overcomers look forward. Overcomers are planners who are organized in their stepping ahead, even if they can only take baby steps. Sometimes, those baby steps guide you through the next thirty minutes, to the next hour, and so on as you continue forward.

My goal in overcoming this situation was to decide what self-talk I would use when this incident came to mind. Although it has been many years since I honestly thought about this incident, in the beginning, it was negative—I wondered what I had done wrong and berated myself for not telling anyone. Through healing, I started to tell myself it wasn't my fault; I did nothing to encourage this situation. Over the years, I could finally take a deep breath and remind myself, *I forgive Frank for what he did.*

These personal stories helped me become the overcomer that I am. I'm sharing them to let you know that we are all overcomers. Every situation that happens to us occurs for some reason. There's always a GLOW—gifts, lessons, opportunities, and wisdom to be gained from each situation that occurs in our lives. After I learned about this abuse, what changed for me? I can recognize that I now relate more intimately to people in my life. My heart feels freer.

When the event occurred when I was three, there was no GLOW, but it's always there, waiting to be uncovered. A lesson is that I am more aware of the possibility of abuse, and an opportunity is my ability to protect little ones better. A gift is that I am a better person after reaching the other side of a traumatic situation. There's wisdom in sharing my experience with other mothers, including the importance of teaching children the difference between good touch and bad touch. There's a gift in realizing this information later in life when I was better equipped to navigate it.

I can only control my thoughts and actions today; what am I thinking and doing now? Worrying about the past or the future will not benefit me in any way. It was okay for me to do nothing with this information for a few years. I held the information at bay because I wanted to do that, and I planned to process it when I was ready. It was a conscious choice.

The key to being an overcomer is listening to and processing your thoughts. Take them in or push them out, but don't dwell on them. Take action or do nothing, but be aware of your choice. When thoughts come into your mind, process them, listen to them, and decide what you will do with them. Ideas come and go—thousands and thousands every day. We get to decide which thoughts we want to hold on to and which thoughts we want to act on. These choices happen fast, but it is always up to us to choose. What will you choose? Being an overcomer means you choose to live in the present and don't keep looking in the rearview mirror.

Lessons Learned:

- When a traumatic event occurs, we may block it from our memory until we are ready to heal.

- Working through trauma requires a conscious effort.

- Our brains can suppress traumatic events, but our cells remember.

- There is no easy path to getting over child sexual abuse; acknowledging that it occurred is the first step.

- Understanding and accepting that it's not your fault is the key to overcoming trauma.

- Continually reflect and move forward.

- Healing from sexual abuse takes time, understanding, and forgiveness.

- Every situation that happens to us occurs for a reason.

- I can only control my thoughts and actions today.

- Listen to your thoughts and consciously decide what you will do with them.

Overcoming
Rape

Some people believe there's no such thing as rape if you're married, but "no" always means "no," whether you're married or not. Certain men don't hear that word; they feel like their wives are there to do with what they want. This was not my idea of an ideal marriage.

He was drunk, and so was I—not an unusual occurrence in our rocky marriage. By this time, we had three children and had been married for eight years. I often tried to avoid getting into bed at the same time as him because our sexual encounters had become unpleasant. I hoped he would go to bed first; then I could make some excuse to stay up. Usually, that gave me time to have another drink to ensure I would sleep soundly next to the person I was growing so far apart from.

We did go to bed together on that fateful night. I slowly slunk into bed and rolled over to my usual sleeping position, my back facing him, clinging tightly to my side of the bed and breathing slowly, sometimes covering my mouth, as if it would make a difference. Staring mindlessly out the window into the night sky, I imagined I was somewhere else, on a beach, in a cabana, happily exhausted, having just finished intimately dancing the night away together. Reality stings.

On this particular night, he grabbed my shoulder and rolled me onto my back without a word. I quietly and calmly gave the excuse that I was tired, but it didn't work. The groping began. I whispered, "No." I repeated it multiple times, but nothing stopped him. He was big and heavy. His breath stunk like old beer, and his grunting was inescapable. I reminded myself that if I lie still, it would be over quickly. I never understood how he could enjoy this when I was acting like a dead fish, but he never seemed to mind.

The Bible tells us that wives must obey their husbands and be subservient. However, it also says the husband should treat the wife with respect: "Wives, submit to your own husbands, as to the Lord. For the husband is the head of the wife even as Christ is the head of the church, his body, and is himself its Savior. Now as the church submits to Christ, so also wives should submit in everything to their husbands. Husbands love your wives, as Christ loved the church and gave himself up for her, that he might sanctify her, having cleansed her by the washing of water with the word" (Ephesians 5:22-23, NIV).

I believe that this verse is often taken out of context and used to justify domestic violence. We were put on this Earth to procreate. That creation should be a beautiful, loving act. Once the act becomes full of rage and anger, it becomes tainted.

We glide through the ocean water in ankle-deep waves. As we stop to glance at the full moon, he gently caresses my soft face, slowly slides his strong hand down the back of my neck, and wraps my long, flowing hair around his fingers. He gently pushes the hair away from my face and leans in to press his soft lips against mine in a hot, gentle kiss. The moonlight shines bright as we embrace each other in sheer delight. Our bodies sway in unison as my hands slowly slide over his muscular shoulders and down to the small of his back. He slowly disrobes me. I gently squeeze his buttocks as I slide his khakis off. Our breathing becomes heavier. Our eyes meet in the moonlight, and permission is given. We are in unison and deeply in love. We kiss passionately, our tongues touching and flitting. We breathe into each other's mouths as we gently lie in the surf. The crashing water feels fantastic on our naked skin. Our deep breaths are in sync, uniting our souls. We continue this breathing and caressing technique until we are both in a very relaxed state of mind. Our hands continue to caress and grope each other, touching all parts of our extremities. We tease along the way, just brushing past those climactic parts. We continue in this very sensual, loving, sexual act. I slowly slip on top of him and feel his pulsing. We both wriggle in delight, switching to multiple positions until we have exhausted ourselves. My mind is far away from the angry male who has thrown himself on top of me, pinning my arms over my head. Despite his drunken state, he tries his best to finish the act.

This unloving act occurred on multiple occasions. My self-talk around this was always negative, driven by shame and guilt: *Why don't I just accept my husband's wishes? What is my problem? I am supposed to do this. This is the true purpose of marriage. We love each other; that's why we got married. And if I had just not had that last drink, things might have gone a lot better. I need to listen to him and do what he asks; then everything will be much better.* But I never believed those words. Deep down inside, I have always been a strong-willed, obstinate person with deep values and beliefs. I knew I had lost myself in that marriage and let the relationship dwindle to nothingness. I also knew I always have three options:

1. Stay right where I am, don't change a thing, and maintain the status quo.

2. Have some conversations, compromise, and see what I can do to make things better.

3. Get out and run.

These options are always available: stay, negotiate, or leave. No one can make me do or feel anything. I can fight harder, scream, and kick. I did not want to do the hard work necessary to keep that relationship alive, but ultimately, I considered my three children sleeping on the other side of the wall. So, I chose to be quiet, accept his disrespectful behavior, and let it ride until it subsided. Even though I chose to be subservient, at no point should you feel obligated to stay with an abuser—you are not responsible for your abuser's behavior, nor did you cause it. We always choose what is in our best interest at any given moment, and back then, I believed that addressing the broken relationship

I had with my husband would hurt the relationship I have with my children. I honored my relationship with my children more than my own peace.

It is easy to roll over and play the victim, especially when these are my realities: I was sexually abused at three years old. I was physically abused with a belt by my biological father, who abandoned me at seven years old. Multiple stepfathers walked in and out of my life. My marriage was riddled with emotional and physical abuse. Not only did my husband rape me numerous times but he also committed adultery. I had never seen what a healthy relationship looks like. I could have sat and wallowed in my unhealthy marriage. Poor me—I am the victim, and there's nothing I can do about it. This is just my life, it sucks, and I'm stuck with it.

Dwelling on those thoughts is a choice, one that many people continue to make. Some people choose this forever. Choice Theory reminds us that all behavior is purposeful, and we are all doing the best we can at any given moment. If we genuinely believe that, then the next minute, something different can happen, or the same thing can happen.

Henry Ford once said, "Whether you think you can or can't, you're right." If I believed I could never get out of my abusive marriage, that would be true. If I thought I could get out someday, that would be true. If I believed I was getting out of this relationship within a year, then that would be true. I did think about getting out for about four years. Once I changed my thinking and made a real plan, I was finally able to act.

My plan to escape took more than twelve months to implement because it had to be carefully put in place. My safety and the safety of my children were at risk. We did have guns in the house. My husband had said on more than one occasion, "I will kill you if you leave," "You'll never see the children again," "You'll never see the light of day again," and "You can't go far enough away, I'll always find you." These statements are strong, and they stayed with me. If I believed all my negative self-talk, I would have continued to stay in my marriage because *whatever thou thinkest, thou shalt be.*

Overcoming situations that seem out of our control or are not our fault can be very challenging. I would posit that the first step is to avoid victim thinking. Stay away from the blame game. Stay away from the disconnecting habits of blaming, nagging, criticizing, complaining, threatening, punishing, and bribing. And when you falter, don't beat yourself up about it anymore. All that shame and guilt is just wasting space in your head. I used to beat myself up and say, *I can't believe it. Why did you do that? What were you thinking? You're never going to get what you need or where you need to go.* Those thoughts only point me in the direction I don't want to go.

Most importantly, be sure to accept responsibility for all your actions. Everything that occurs in my life is my responsibility, and I can choose whether I will stay and do nothing, stick around and work on a compromise, or get out. Every step I take is my choice, and I am responsible for going in that direction. Wow, that is a difficult fact to swallow.

When you are faced with a situation you must overcome, be strong and courageous. When you find yourself in the wrong place at the wrong time, consciously decide to let it be or get out. Bad things do happen to good people; you were in the wrong place at the wrong time. Move on, don't wallow in it. Get out of the victim's mindset. Take responsibility for your actions. You are an overcomer. I am an overcomer. We will persist with our goals and overcome the adversities ahead of us.

Lessons Learned:

- Ephesians 5:22-23 is often taken out of context.

- I can stay, negotiate, or leave. It is up to me. I have choices.

- No one can make me do or feel anything.

- We always choose what is in our best interest at any given moment.

- There is always a GLOW—gifts, lessons, opportunities, and wisdom.

- My choices have consequences.

- Trust your gut.

- Remember, don't play the victim.

- All behavior is purposeful: We are all doing the very best we can at any given moment with the information we have.

- "Whether you think you can or can't, you're right."

- Stay away from the blame game.

- Stay away from the disconnecting habits of blaming, nagging, criticizing, complaining, threatening, punishing, and bribing.

- Every single thing that occurs in my life is my responsibility.

- Every single step I take in my life is my choice.

- I am responsible for the direction my life takes.

Overcoming a
Disability

Physical, Emotional, Health, Learning

"If I didn't know what it feels like to be broken, then how would I know what it feels like to be whole?" –We Are Messengers, "Maybe it's OK"

During an NPR interview in 2014, *Good Morning America* co-anchor Robin Roberts spoke about her memoir, *Everybody's Got Something.* Whenever Robin would complain about life being unfair, her mother would say, "Oh, honey, everybody's got something." It wasn't until Robin was diagnosed with breast cancer that she understood, "Yes, everybody's got something… my something is no bigger, no more important, not anything more than anybody else's." Even though we might "have" something, we also have something to give back: hope, encouragement, an organ, blood, bone marrow, and so on.

Robin's "something" was not only breast cancer; she was also diagnosed with myelodysplastic syndrome, a rare blood disorder that required a bone marrow transplant. As a public figure, Robin was courageous enough to share her trials and triumphs with her audience. Once, I heard her say, "As my mother always says: 'Make your mess your message.'" What a great message to live by.

I've got something. It was June of 1998. I was a thirty-five-year-old woman working as a classroom aide in a high school setting, recently separated from my husband of twelve years. I had moved to my own apartment with my two nine-year-old twin girls and a six-year-old son. My salary was $6.25 an hour. I honestly had no idea how to make anything work financially, so I knew I needed to change.

There were only a few more days before the school year ended. I was talking to the special education teacher I worked with when I suddenly felt dizzy. I began to say, "I've never felt this dizzy in all my—"

That's all I remember. Next, I awoke to a scared special education teacher yelling to another teacher in the hallway to get the nurse and call 9-1-1. I was looking at the ceiling, wondering why everybody was so concerned.

Soon, there was an EMT in my face. "Can you hear me? Are you OK?" As I looked around to get my bearings, I realized I was lying on the floor in the hallway of the school I worked in.

"Are you incontinent?" That was a strange, dumb question; why would he ask such a thing? I reached down to feel my dress to find it was drenched in urine. Then he said, "I used to be in special education. I don't know how to spell the word incontinent. Can you help me?"

I started to laugh, but nobody else was laughing. Then I realized I couldn't feel my arms and legs. The only things that were functioning were my head, my eyes, and my mouth. I saw the worry on their faces. I heard them say that my blood pressure was a crazy high number. Nobody quite knew what to do with me.

They loaded me onto the stretcher and took me to the nearest hospital. This occurred around 9:30 in the morning. I spent the next few hours in the emergency room, watching nurses come and go from my room with a look of worry on their faces, anxiously checking the beeping machinery beside my bed.

I didn't know it then, but my heart was beating way too fast. I was having way too many premature ventricular contractions (PVCs)—runs of three, four, and five in a row. Nobody likes to see those kinds of heartbeats. After giving me some medication, they waited for my heart to return to a normal rhythm—but it wasn't happening.

Then, the doctor was at my bedside, very concerned. "Are you afraid of helicopters?" he asked.

I said, "Well, that's a silly question. I love helicopters. I've never been in one. Where am I going?"

He said, "We need to transport you on the Life Star helicopter to a different hospital that can help deal with your heart condition. We are very worried about you."

I always use humor as a defense mechanism, so I was jovial with the nurses, joking about the situation. The doctor told me I had better not be this jovial with Life Star EMTs because they took their work very seriously. I realized that most patients who ride in the Life Star helicopter are usually unconscious. Here I am, feeling normal, not in any pain. I was a little lightheaded, but other than that, I was feeling good, even though I couldn't stand up. Over the hospital's loudspeaker, I heard them tell everyone to clear their cars from the parking lot because the Life Star helicopter would be landing any minute. It was surreal.

The Life Star EMTs came rushing into my room, just like you see on television. They whisked me from the emergency room gurney to their travel gurney and strapped me down with huge seatbelts across my chest, belly, and legs. It was very confining. No words were spoken. Their every move was precise and speedy.

Then we were on the move, running down the hallway and through the parking lot where a large crowd had gathered, my special education teacher and two of my high school students among them. My hands were strapped down tightly, but I could lift my hand at the wrist and wave to them. Tears welled up in my eyes. I wanted to be brave, but deep down, I was so frightened.

As I was wheeled through the parking lot, more than thirty students and staff were waiting to see me off. It was then that I realized how serious my condition was. As I was loaded into the Life Star, I remember looking up at the helicopter blades whirring speedily above me and wondering what would happen if I caught my hair in them. The stretcher fits perfectly horizontally in the helicopter, with just enough room for two EMTs to monitor my vital signs during the twelve-minute ride.

When we were airborne, I thought of my children. I assumed I would be in and out of the emergency room in plenty of time to meet them after school. Realizing I wouldn't be there to pick them up, I grew frantic.

As a single mother with three kids, all the responsibility fell on me. My ex-husband would not get them; I had to think of someone else.

In the late '90s, cell phones were not as available as now. The EMTs saw my fear and connected me with my friend during the helicopter ride. I explained my situation: "I am in the Life Star helicopter right now, on my way to the hospital, and I am not going to be able to pick up my kids. Can you help me out?"

Melissa replied, "Only you, Lois! Of course, I can help."

The helicopter landed just as swiftly as it had taken off. Once again, I was hustled out of the helicopter and rushed into the hospital. I had no idea I would spend the next two weeks there.

As they conducted test after test, the medical staff told me they had not seen anything like this. The tilt test was particularly horrible. In preparation, they put removable sticky defibrillator pads on the front and back of my chest in case they had to shock my body to stop my heartbeat. (When your heart is beating too fast, it needs a shock to come out of fibrillation, hence the term "defibrillation.") It is a jolt of 200 to 360 joules of electricity, and it feels like a horse kicking you in the chest. They call it therapeutic intervention; I call it shock therapy. Then they stood me up at an eighty-degree angle on a board and put me on oxygen. Looking back on it now, it felt like a torture chamber.

They injected some drugs into my system that made my heart beat faster and faster and faster. It felt like I was having a real heart attack. My left arm was numb, and I felt like I was going to throw up. I told them that I thought I was going to die. The doctor kept saying, "Don't worry, don't worry, you're going to be fine." But then mayhem broke out, and the doctor started shouting, "Stop the test! Lie her down!"

They left me there to collect myself while they called over three more doctors who stared at me from the hallway in awe, whispering and pointing at me. I later discovered that I had experienced a run of thirteen PVCs, but despite this, I had not passed out. They did not know why. They decided to put me on a clinical trial medication, and three days later, they did the test again. I cried and asked them not to, but they said it would be different this time—and it was. It was unremarkable. Nothing happened. They were delighted, and so was I.

The whole time I was hospitalized, I had to find friends to watch my children and get them to school. It was a very stressful time for all involved.

I was the youngest patient on the heart floor—agile compared to most patients, who were typically older than seventy. They were dying on that floor. Even though they were strangers to me, I visited their rooms to discuss their lives with them. They thanked me, especially because some had never had any visitors.

By the time I could go home, it was mid-June, and school was over. I returned to my empty apartment as a single mother of three kids.

They never labeled my heart problem; they didn't know what it was. The doctor said that I could never have another child. He also told me that by the time I was fifty years old, this progressive degenerative heart disease would debilitate me, and I would most likely need a heart transplant to survive. Then, he discharged me and sent me on my way. A progressive degenerative heart disease—those words stung. Not wanting to accept them, I just looked at my doctor, said, "We'll see," and left. I decided I was going to beat this. I didn't know what it was, but I would fight it.

After I got home, I was determined to be the best mother I could be. I continued to take my heart medication and followed up with my doctor once a year. After two years, he said, "We still don't know what you have, but we want to give you an implanted cardiac defibrillator" (ICD). At this point, I was thirty-seven years old. He said I was very young to have this problem, and they didn't know what it was or how to treat it.

Defibrillators detect life-threatening rapid heart rhythms. If the dangerous rhythm does not stop, the ICD shocks the heart to restore a normal rhythm. Then, the device goes back to its watchful mode.

It was then that I learned why I was still alive. My doctor said, "You're only here because of how hard you fell when you had your seizure; your body was literally jolted back to life." On that fateful day, I had fallen like a tree, straight down, out the door into the hallway. I landed hard enough to jolt my heart out of fibrillation.

Have you ever seen someone take their fist and pound on someone's chest when they are unconscious? That is why—to jolt them.

I said, "Wow, that's pretty cool."

"We don't want that to happen to you again," he explained, "so we want to give you this defibrillator."

Implanting the defibrillator entailed an eight-hour invasive surgery where they fished some wires through the veins in my neck into the top and bottom of my heart. The wires twist directly into the heart tissue like a fishhook. Then they plugged in the defibrillator, a three-square-inch metal computer box weighing two and a half ounces, before sewing me up. I became a thirty-seven-year-old bionic woman with a defibrillator implanted in my body. Living with a device that could shock me at any moment was terrifying.

It took much mental conversation to get out and walk around in public. I always had this underlying feeling that at any given moment, I could fall, and the defibrillator would provide me with "therapy," which, as I said, is like a horse kicking me in the chest with its hind legs. How embarrassing that would be. I could die and come back to life in front of everyone. I was encouraged to attend a support group for people with implanted defibrillators. When I entered the room, there were about ten other people, none younger than seventy. Tears welled in my eyes as I looked around and thought, *Oh my God, what am I doing here?* I had a disabling condition that nobody could see; it felt like I was in an invisible wheelchair. I needed to figure out how to live with it for the rest of my life.

However, I was comforted in my belief that we grow the most during the most challenging times. Can you think of a trying time in your life? Were you able to learn anything from it?

Many people are reading this book right now who are more disabled than I am—me, with my tiny little implanted defibrillator. However, any disabling condition warrants mental discussion. So, I sat around that support group and told my story. Then, I realized I needed to live each day to the fullest—no sitting around crying about it because we never know what tomorrow will bring. Thinking of my condition this way freed me from the chains of "sameness." I realized I needed to live my life, as I had gotten a second chance at it.

When I realized this, I was catapulted into genuinely living, and this condition became a blessing. It would only be as disabling as I made it. Suddenly, I felt like a superwoman, like I could do anything. My life blossomed.

"Get out, live your life, and don't worry. We have our life-saving devices," I said to the support group. "We can go crazy if we want to, and we won't die because this computer will save us!"

That was nearly three decades ago, and I still feel that way. I am over sixty years old now and still ticking. I have not needed a heart transplant (yet), and although my condition isn't getting any better, it isn't getting any worse either. I've had more than eight surgeries, and this defibrillator has defibrillated me five times in my life. Yes, it was in public, and yes, it wasn't very comfortable—but it saved my life. I never let my heart condition impede me in any way. It empowers me.

I will continue to reiterate this often: Our thoughts are so powerful. Our thoughts and actions lead us. As the saying goes, "Whether you think you can or cannot, you are correct." Whatever you think, is.

So, if you are struggling with any disability, you can understand some of the feelings I have discussed. Our bodies are very intricate, and so many physically disabling conditions can occur—from missing limbs and fingers to eyes and ears that don't work correctly, not to mention emotionally disabling conditions such as depression, anxiety, obsessive-compulsive disorder, and neurosis. My condition happens to be electrical and involves my heart, and a heart is just one organ.

If you live with a disability, sit back and reflect: What barriers have you already overcome? What obstacles are still in your path, and how can you get around them? Can you sit with them? My friend Kim Olver works very hard to help people understand that there's always a GLOW—gifts, lessons, opportunities, and wisdom any situation or circumstance brings—because the concept is sometimes hard to believe. Please consider the disabling condition you are experiencing and see if you can unearth the GLOW. Understand that finding the GLOW is difficult at first and takes practice.

My GLOW was centered on the realization that I received a second chance at life as a bionic woman with a life-saving device in my chest. The words we choose make all the difference. My condition is not disabling at all—it is enabling, allowing me to function in the world with no worries.

Over the last ten years, I have gone parachuting over the mountains in France, ziplining over the Las Vegas Strip, and white-water rafting through the Grand Canyon. I have run off mountains in Rio De Janeiro to hang-glide over the Copacabana. I am a firewalker. I've had many crazy adventures, and I never worried about my safety.

I'm not saying you should run off a mountain. I'm just saying that whatever disability you're dealing with, maybe you could see it or label it differently.

I work with students with special needs, and I have spent my whole life advocating for people with special needs. Having a learning disability or an emotional disability is disabling to that person until they uncover all the strengths that come with it. We all have strengths and weaknesses, and we all have experienced trials and triumphs.

It's incredible to realize that my thoughts and actions genuinely guide my emotions and my body's physical reactions. I spent many years struggling and wondering if I could control my heartbeat. A piece of me wants to continue to try to heal my heartbeat and get off my medication, which I never go more than twelve hours without. I always get a little scared if I miss a dose. It is life-threatening, like a person with diabetes not taking insulin. Are you hoping you can find a way to live comfortably with your disabling condition? Can you believe that you are just as you should be? Can you be OK with how you are?

It is possible.

If you don't have a disabling condition, you may have someone in your life who does, and you could help your loved one become more accepting of their condition. In the end, it's not about the label. It's simply about our thoughts and actions and how we accept who we are.

I accept who I am at this moment. I am who I am. I love me.

After reading this chapter, I hope you gain a few skills to assist you in accepting and loving yourself just as you are.

You are beautiful. I can see the GLOW.

LESSONS LEARNED:

- Make your mess your message.

- We grow the most during the most challenging times of our lives.

- My condition was actually a blessing, and it would only be as disabling as I made it.

- Whether you think you can or cannot, you are correct. Whatever you think is, is.

- My thoughts and actions guide my emotions and my body's physical reactions.

- I accept who I am at this moment. I am who I am. I love me.

Overcoming
Infidelity

"The shattering of a heart is the loudest quiet ever." –Carroll Bryant

At the beginning of our young marriage, my ex-husband and I partied together, and I always knew he was flirtatious—but following through was another story. He was a good-looking DJ. I loved him dearly. I confronted him when I found proof of that credit card receipt: an entire bottle of wine and room service for two at a luxurious hotel. I believed him when he told me his side of the story. There was always a story. He said, "Actually, that's not how it went…It was just a friend from high school, and we happened to cross paths. I love you." When you love someone with all your heart, you can be blinded.

I knew it, I felt it, I did not want to believe it, but it was true. We were married for seven years with three children, but he was sleeping with other women—multiple women. And this went on for years.

I loved him so much that, at his request, I went so far as to invite one of these other women into the house. We all sat down to eat dinner and have a conversation, and he proceeded to tell us that he loved both of us. I was aghast. How crazy was I? I wanted to save the marriage. My church did not approve of divorce. I did not want to be a divorced woman. I wanted to celebrate my fiftieth wedding anniversary with the love of my life. I kept trying and trying, even though I wasn't sure if I could ever forgive him. However, I could not envision getting divorced and being a single parent with three children, and I liked the financial stability the marriage afforded me. Over the next five years, the infidelity continued. I looked the other way, and alcohol became my new partner. Vodka was my alcohol of choice and my new best friend. It doesn't smell and can be mixed with many things, numbing my feelings. I would put the kids to bed and start my drinking routine, drowning my sorrows in alcohol. I did not want to get in bed while he was still awake. This lifestyle continued for several years until it spun out of control.

Infidelity is very painful to experience. It creates a lot of shame. Why would my husband go after someone else when I was right there beside him? Was something wrong with me? Was I too fat, too short, too ugly? These thoughts were all-consuming. This negative self-talk was all about the outer shell of my being. My inner, loving soul disappeared under the veil of alcohol as I became a quiet, functioning closet drinker.

Eventually, I turned outside of the marriage to have my own affair. I did not consciously decide to have an affair; I believe my underlying subconscious was looking for ways to get revenge. I was so competitive that I couldn't let my husband beat me. I was so hurt that I had to act, and it just happened. Affairs don't start in the bedroom; they begin with the small things. I don't ever remember wanting to hurt my husband. Part of me felt like I just wanted to know what it feels like to experience infidelity from the other side. I remember thinking, *He had his affair, and he's probably having affairs right now, so it's okay for me to have this affair.* For about six months, I was walking in unknown territory, and it was both fun and scary.

Sneaking around is an exciting thing, meeting in quiet places you would never usually meet, and making sure that nobody would suspect anything based on your schedule. One of the hardest things was keeping track of the lies I told—lies about where I was and why I came home late for the babysitter. I tried my best to stick to the story at all costs, but just like I had confronted him about his infidelity when he was drinking, one night, he confronted me about my affair.

I arrived home at four o'clock in the morning after I'd been drinking. I thought I would sneak into the house without a trace and quietly slip into bed undetected. My heart sank when I saw my husband sitting on the couch with his best male friend, legs crossed, beers in hand. Not only does alcohol give us loose lips but it also hinders our ability to remember the details of our lives—especially when they're lies. I think I finally just wanted to let it go. Many hurtful words were said, punches were thrown, and I vowed to leave the marriage for good.

Infidelity is a behavior. We all behave in the best way we know how at any given moment. Both parties in a relationship need to take responsibility for their part in the infidelity. As I am currently in a healthy, loving marriage, infidelity has never crossed my mind, and I completely trust that it has not crossed my current husband's mind. Infidelity is something that helps people in a relationship understand that their connection is broken. One or both partners choose infidelity as a coping behavior because it's the only thing they can think of to meet their needs.

We all choose behaviors to fulfill our needs, and if we can't do that within a relationship, we will look outside the relationship for something that will help us meet those needs. It took me many years to realize I was responsible for a piece of my ex-husband's infidelity. I took part in allowing the relationship to crumble, and he chose a coping behavior of infidelity to meet his needs. I am not blaming myself for my ex-husband having an affair; I am simply taking some responsibility for the relationship falling apart. In a healthy, loving relationship, these thoughts never cross our minds. When I was in that marriage, I could not imagine what a healthy relationship looked like.

I grew up in a family of dysfunctional marriage role models. Although I was not privy to any infidelity in the marriages of my mom or my siblings, I do know that my mother was divorced seven times, my oldest sister was divorced twice and remains single, my next brother down is in his fourth marriage, my next sister raised three kids she had with three different men as a single parent, my next sister did not marry until she was in her late forties and was extremely unhappy in that relationship, my younger sister married twice, I'm on my third marriage, and my youngest brother became a devoted Mormon on his eighteenth birthday and never looked back. He is now building his own

Mormon church family, with a long-standing wife of thirty-two years, four children, five grandchildren, and the Mormon church as their rock. What I'm trying to say is that my siblings and I never experienced examples of loving, healthy, genuine, authentic relationships between two adults. I did not realize what it looked like or felt like to have a healthy, loving, monogamous relationship.

We were high school sweethearts. I saw his anger from when he was sixteen. I still married the nineteen-year-old I thought I could change. I was sure his anger would disappear if I loved him enough and showed him what a wonderful person I was. Plus, the anger couldn't possibly continue when we had children. But things never did get better. When you combine anger with alcohol, things get very messy. Then, add infidelity on top of that, and the relationship crumbles. I remember the pain and the agony I felt when I first found out he was cheating on me. I wanted to control him and his drinking, his anger, and his infidelity. I still truly believed I could change those behaviors.

As I stated before, I was very comfortable being taken care of financially. I waitressed on the weekends, but I could never imagine finding a house, paying rent, paying all the bills, and raising three kids on my own. When you don't have a vision, you don't have a goal. You can't get anywhere if you don't know where you're headed. I truly believed I was doomed to stay in this unhealthy, unloving atmosphere because I had no other choice. It is that kind of thinking that keeps us down.

My ex-husband was brought up with fear hanging over his head at every turn. That is how his parents raised him, so that is how he chose to be in a relationship with me—hanging fear over my head at every turn. I now understand he was behaving the best way he knew how. He kept me locked in the relationship with statements like, "I will kill you if you leave," or, "You'll never be able to make it on your own. You have three kids. How do you think you're going to feed them?" or, "You'll never see any child support from me," or, "I'll come to find you, and you will be sorry."

If I wanted to break free, I realized I had to get a more stable job. I was excited to be hired as a classroom paraeducator in our local high school. When I announced my new appointment to my husband, he said, "That's not a real job. That's just playing with kids." Six years later, I proudly walked across the lit-up graduation stage, sporting my floppy doctoral graduation hat, and received my doctoral degree in educational leadership. I eventually landed my dream job at the top of the heap: Dr. Lois C. Knapton, public school superintendent—a "real" job!

Once I started to believe in myself, I was able to make progress. We don't know what we don't know. We only know what we do know. Since I had never seen a healthy relationship, I truly believed I was destined to live my life in this unhealthy relationship. I watched my ex-husband's parents live out their unhealthy marriage (in my perception) with a subservient wife and a fear-mongering husband. I thought that was normal. In my mid-thirties, I started to question my marriage. When the infidelity finally came to light, I started reading books, asking questions, and seeking out counselors who could help me work through my feelings and help me decide what direction to head in.

If you are struggling with infidelity, you have three choices— as always: You can leave things precisely the way they are and do nothing, you can change things and work on the relationship, or you can remove yourself from the relationship. You always have a choice, and each choice has consequences. If you're having trouble figuring out what you want for yourself, sit quietly and ask yourself, "What would you have if you magically had everything you wanted right now?"

A famous Henry Ford quote states, "Whether you think you can, or you think you can't, you're right." You truly are what you think. If you think you can, you're right. If you feel you can't, you're right. Words are so powerful; our self-talk is what can keep us down and raise us up. As you navigate the experience of infidelity, you can still be satisfied with who you are. Don't beat yourself up—realize that you are doing the best you can right now, and if you don't like what that looks like or what that feels like, you can choose to change.

The critical thing to remember is that you, indeed, are amazing. You can achieve things you never thought were possible. We can all get what we want. You might not believe that is a true statement, especially if you are living in an unhealthy marriage, but if you believe everyone behaves in the best way possible to meet their needs, then you are in the best place at any given moment. If you feel out of balance, you have those three choices discussed earlier: accept, negotiate, or leave. Be courageous, set your goals, and take that first step. Before you know it, you'll be somewhere you never thought you would be.

Lesson Learned:

- Infidelity is a behavior, and we all choose the best behavior that we know at that moment to meet our needs.

- Both parties in a relationship need to take responsibility for their part in the infidelity.

- Infidelity is a coping behavior that can help people in a relationship understand that their connection is broken.

- We all behave to fulfill our needs, and if our current relationship is not fulfilling our needs, we will look outside the relationship for something that will help us meet those needs.

- You can't get anywhere if you don't know where you're going.

- You always have three choices: do nothing, leave, or negotiate.

- You can achieve things you never thought were possible.

- You are what you think.

OVERCOMING
Divorce

"Incredible change happens in your life when you decide to take control of what you do have power over instead of craving control over what you don't." –Steve Maraboli

I always pictured myself on my fiftieth wedding anniversary. That's one of the reasons why I never wanted to get divorced. I was also clinging to skewed Christian belief: the Lord hated divorce. I eventually realized he meant he didn't like the state of divorce; he never said he hates the people who get divorced. Divorce is not an unforgivable sin. Divorce is simply a sin like any other sin in the Bible, and God forgives sinners.

I am in my third marriage. Unfortunately, I did not have a healthy role model regarding relationships, and my past marriages were abusive and unfaithful. I watched my mother divorce and remarry seven times. I don't blame anything on them. I don't play the victim. I use this information to help me remember what I want and don't want. Finally, after my second divorce at forty-one years old, I realized that I needed to be clear on what I wanted. I wanted a healthy, committed, unconditionally loving adult relationship.

When I was seven, my mom divorced my biological father after being married for nineteen years with seven children. My father was abusive to his family, and I will never forget the nighttime routine of lashings. Back then, it was just my life, but now I often wonder why my mother allowed that to happen to her children. Beyond the abuse, memories of my biological father are minimal, though I recall eating popcorn with him while he watched television and drank whiskey. His breath always had that whiskey smell. Then, one day, my mother piled all seven children in the old station wagon and moved an hour away. She met another man, Bernie, and got married. He was my first stepfather, and I always considered him my "real dad." She stayed married to him for seven years. Bernie was an alcoholic who yelled a lot and had favorites. Thankfully, I was one of the favorites. My other siblings, not so much. He would drag them around by their hair, yank on their ears, throw things at them, and kick the teenage kids in their butts. The other siblings would gawk, glad the attack was not meant for them that day.

Despite the divorce, I stayed in contact with Bernie until the day he died. He loved my mother dearly, but alcohol always gets the best of any relationship, and he could not put down the glass. That was divorce number two—the one that hit me the hardest.

I was fourteen years old, a freshman in high school, when my mother got married for the third time. Stepfather number two, Gene, owned a campground and invited us there for the summer. My younger brother ran away years ago to live with our biological father. All my siblings were older and already out of the house, so it was just me and my younger sister, Susan. It sounded like a beautiful way to spend the summer until we realized we were free labor for Gene. We had to clean the cabins after people left, mow the lawns, and do all the laundry. It was one of the worst times in my life. My mother was blinded by this seemingly charming gentleman using her children for slave labor. We felt trapped.

One night, I heard a lot of yelling downstairs, and I decided I would no longer be a bystander; my mother needed protection. I ran down the stairs just in time to see her get smacked across the face and fall to the ground. I jumped between them, screaming for Gene to stop. To this day, I don't know where I got that courage because he was big. I was only 5'4" and fourteen years old, but I stood my ground. My mother crouched on the ground as her third husband continued to yell at her. I said, "Mom, we're leaving," and he said, "The hell you are!" But we packed our bags, got in the car, and drove away. Divorce number three occurred.

Thankfully, my mother never went back.

I felt frustrated and embarrassed that my mother couldn't stay married. Entering my second year in high school, I had been dating a guy for longer than she had been married. Kids at school made fun of me because my mom liked to "sleep around."

By the time I was a junior, my mother had married another guy and got married. I never watched how she built these relationships with the men she would marry, but looking back now, I believe they lacked a solid foundation. I asked my mother why she kept getting married; why couldn't she just date? She said, "I was brought up very proper and can't have sexual relations unless I am married," and left it at that. We are guided by the values and morals our parents teach us. Sometimes, they guide us in the wrong direction, away from our goals.

Stepdad number three was Vinny. My mother's fourth marriage lasted four years. He was a disabled veteran, and my mother was very excited because she got GI Bill money for me when I was in college. I remember receiving monthly checks of $250. Back then, it was a tremendous amount of money. I always felt guilty taking this money because I wasn't his kid and didn't even know this guy. I also didn't like him, but at least he wasn't violent. Nonetheless, she eventually divorced him.

The cycle of abuse ramped up with Jerry, an angry alcoholic— my mother's fifth husband, my fourth stepfather. At nineteen years old, I quit college and married my high school sweetheart. I often got phone calls from my sobbing mother, stuck on the roadside or in some crazy, unsafe situation. I will never forget when she told me she was sleeping with a gun under her pillow because she feared for her life. No child needs to hear this kind of story from her mother. Eventually, she and Jerry got divorced, but my mother was unable to be alone. She had met a man who was just a little older than me then and was dating him. To me, it was just gross. My mother was sixty-two years old, and her boyfriend was forty. I had just turned thirty. Seeing my mother acting a lot younger than she was was bizarre. Thankfully, she never married him.

The cycle of abuse is very addictive. Jerry, stepfather number four, the crazy one, lured my mother back into his arms. She remarried the same man; he became stepfather number five and marriage number six. As always, time went by, and she got divorced again. I no longer had to anxiously await a panicked phone call with my frantic mother sobbing hysterically. When she was seventy-five, she remarried and stayed married to my last stepfather, number six, Ken, until he passed away five years later. He was an ornery old man, and they never seemed to get along. My mother passed away at ninety years old. She was a single woman living in a one-bedroom apartment in an assisted living facility. Some of her children would visit her, and some did not speak to her.

During my college days, I still loved my high-school sweetheart. However, we had broken up for a little while, and we both went our separate ways in search of greener pastures. I surely sowed my oats. During my sophomore year in college, he wanted to get back together with me. He had joined the Marine Corps, and he lured me in. I quit school, married, and moved with him to live near Cherry Point Marine Corps Air Station in North Carolina. My family and his family were upset; we did it nonetheless. He was nineteen, and I was twenty. I thought I knew it all.

My marriage to him lasted twelve years. Initially, it was fabulous, fun-loving, and ritualistic due to the Marine Corps lifestyle. But things are not always what they seem. During one of his first deployments, I vividly remember being propositioned by a young Marine. He wanted to sleep with me, and I emphatically said "no." He replied, "Do you think your husband stays faithful out there?" In my naivety, I said "yes," truly believing he was being faithful. I will never know the truth. We loved each other the only way we knew how. He was funny. He was brilliant, handsome, and a hard worker. He was a disc jockey and was very flirtatious. He was also angry, abusive, unfaithful, and yelled a lot. He likes to drink beer. He did a lot of shoving and pulling on the children and me. I always thought I could change him, but it never worked. I knew I was not modeling a healthy relationship for my children. I realized I was living in the same kind of relationship I was trying to protect my mother from. My kids were watching it right in front of their eyes. I often told the children to go to their rooms when Daddy acted up. I was careful not to say that Daddy was a bad person; it was his behavior that was bad. Through therapy, I decided to examine myself: I was controlling. I was using alcohol as a crutch, and I was in denial. One thing is obvious: I am responsible for everything in my life. I will preface that I am responsible for almost everything in my life, except for the incident that occurred with me when I was just three years old and so innocent—I do not feel responsible for that.

Nonetheless, as an adult, I needed to take responsibility for my actions. I have the ability to choose which relationships to stay in and which to leave. I believe that effective relationships are very, very challenging and worth the work. It is a two-way street, so I felt very torn. Around year seven of my first marriage, I discovered my husband had been cheating for years. Just a one-time thing, he said. I stayed for five more years, dragging out this horrible, irreparable relationship. We tried to work it out; he went to counseling, I went to counseling, and we tried to do couples counseling. In the end, nothing worked, and I left. He married the nineteen-year-old girlfriend he was dating at the end of our marriage. I was thirty-five years old. I stayed single and raised three kids until they were in high school. Then my mom connected me with my ex-stepbrother, Dylan, my stepfather Bernie's son. For some reason, this man swept me off my feet. He wasn't a knight in shining armor. He was penniless and unattractive, but I fell for him. After only six months of dating, I was asking God to show me a sign that I was on the right track. If I asked God for a nearly impossible sign, I would never get the sign. So I said, "God, if this man gives me purple flowers for my birthday, I will marry him." And what did I get for my birthday? A dozen purple daisies. God answered my prayers and fulfilled my wish, and we got married. My sister was livid. How can anyone marry their ex-stepbrother?

Three months into our new marriage, we took a twelve-hour road trip to Nova Scotia to visit my ex-in-laws with two fifteen-year-old twin girls and a twelve-year-old son. That vacation showed me that there was no way this man and I would ever stay connected in a marriage. It had only been three months since we'd been married, and I knew it was the biggest mistake I'd ever made. At that point in my life, we needed each other. I needed him to fill a specific role because I was tired of being a single mom. Life was hard for me, and as I look back on it, I realize I used him for what he could give me. I stayed married to him for four years until my girls graduated from high school, and I graduated with my doctoral degree. He was another furious man. Thankfully, his physical abuse was limited to head-butting and punching walls, but the verbal and emotional abuse was constant. It became a game of walking on eggshells, not breaking any of them, and trying to get into bed without him waking up. It's incredible how resilient one becomes. Once again, I wondered how I got here. What was I thinking? According to William Glasser's Choice Theory, I was doing the best I knew how to do at that time. I was doing the best I could with the information I had. We are all doing the very best we can at any given moment. Don't ever forget that. You, too, are doing the very best you know how to.

He needed me as much as I needed him. I knew I could not have any deep conversations regarding emotion with this man, but we sometimes had intellectual conversations. He made significant gains with his career and was able to mend his soured relationships with his children. We assisted his children and allowed his grandchildren to live in our house while their parents improved. Although there were advantages for both of us to stay in the relationship, divorce was inevitable. After that, I vowed never to get married again. I vowed to be a single woman walking this Earth in faith.

I didn't realize I was trying to overcome divorce, but I was. Getting divorced leaves a mark on your heart and mind. I know I can only control myself, so when I am in a relationship with someone, I need to self-evaluate and look at my contributions to the relationship. We never know who we will connect with if we keep an open mind and have explicit goals.

In my quest for answers, I picked up a copy of *Secrets of Happy Couples: Loving Yourself, Your Partner, and Your Life* by my friend,

Kim Olver. The book's first chapter is about the importance of loving yourself. It was time for me to examine who I am for myself, who I am for others, and what I want in life. I wanted a loving relationship. According to the Law of Attraction, you will attract into your life whatever you focus on; whatever you give your energy and attention to will come back to you. I know the importance of being clear on what you want, so I thought long and hard: What would it look like if I had the loving relationship I wanted?

Kim's book encourages people to go out and do the things they love to do. I love to dance. I did ballet and jazz until high school, when I started doing sports. As an adult, I danced with my mom and my first husband. I had taken some ballroom dancing lessons as a single woman, and I decided, after reading her book, not to sit at home. No more, "Poor me, I have no partner. I can't go dancing." I decided to find some adult dances I could go to safely. I found a singles dance for adults forty-plus years old. It was in a big ballroom, and there were about two hundred people there. There was a DJ, dinner, and dessert. It was like attending a wedding reception every weekend without the bride and groom. Lots of people knew each other, and I started to make connections. I went to these dances for two years, enjoying myself, having a great time, meeting people, and dancing with many women. Men were always hanging around the edges waiting to "pick up" the girls, but I never went home with anyone but myself. Some men only wanted one thing, but I made some great female friends.

One Friday night, while at the dance, I was seated at a table with some girlfriends. I spotted a short, spry man dancing to his heart's desire, alone on the dance floor without a care. He was jumping around on the dance floor like the Energizer Bunny, joyful and self-confident. He was utterly alone and in his own world. I asked my friend if she knew him. She said, "Oh, that's Aurelio, he dances with anyone or no one. He doesn't care."

Once I caught his eye, I took my two fingers and pointed back and forth between my eyes and his eyes, as if to say, *I see you, and you see me.* Still sitting at my table, I jiggled my shoulders cha-cha style, side to side, using my body language to entice him to dance with me. He nodded and motioned me over with his hand, so I went and danced with him all night. I came to find out that this perfect stranger was from Brazil, a place I knew nothing about, and only spoke broken English. We spent the next nine months in and out of each other's lives. I eventually told him I didn't want to get wound up in a relationship because I was going to go live in Africa to do some mission work. That was fine because he was going to his home country for the birth of his grandchild. After two months, he returns, and we meet for another month or so.

I was totally hooked on this man. I loved him deeply, but I was so scared to tell him because I didn't think it was real. It couldn't happen. He was madly in love with me, too. In the beginning, I was afraid it was just lust—that sweep-you-off-your-feet lustful kind of love. I didn't know this kind of genuine and authentic love was accessible; I had never experienced this feeling in my whole life. Nothing about this person bothered me—and it bothered me to think that nothing about him bothered me!

Then, I went off on my three-month mission in Africa, and I felt very dedicated to the Bible when I returned. I think my mother's words were stuck in my brain: "You can't have sexual relations unless you're married." I said to this new lover of mine that we can only have sexual relations if we get married. He looked at me funny because that wasn't the case when I first met him—all of a sudden, I'm a woman of faith? To my surprise, he said OK.

Wanting to make sure that this relationship would work, I made a life-changing decision. I decided I did not want to be controlling, especially in relationships. When it comes to controlling others, Glasser's Choice Theory discusses four situations: when you try to force someone else to do something they don't want to do, when someone tries to make you do something you don't want to do, when you and someone else are both trying to make each other do what neither wants to do, and when you are trying to force yourself to do something that you find very painful. I consciously decided to stop trying to control others. Doing so allowed me to move forward with Aurelio.

This was not a way to catch him or to make him marry me. I committed to not being controlling in my relationships, but I had this powerful urge to follow Biblical principles around sex. I had a conversation with my minister about it. As I look back on it, it seems crazy, but for the next eight months, we followed that conviction. We were celibate together, and it was an amazing way to build a relationship. We got engaged in Rio de Janeiro and are still married to this day. We are absolutely in love, and it's the best thing ever. Overcoming is real.

An overcomer is someone who can take any situation and turn it into something good. There is always a silver lining—we just have to be mindful and seek out that silver lining. It truly is there for all of us in every situation. There is a GLOW: gifts, lessons, opportunities, and wisdom to discover in every one of our life-changing experiences. People and things come into our lives for a season or a reason. It is our job to assess this continually. We can't see what is ahead if we are always looking in our rearview mirror. It is critically important to set goals for yourself, not dwell in the past, not get stuck in victimhood, not let others tell you how you should feel, and not let others tell you what you should be doing. It would be best if you were doing what you want to be doing. Figure out what you want and go for it. Know that you can have it because you are an overcomer.

Lessons Learned:

- Our upbringing, the values, and morals our parents teach us guide our lives.
- I am responsible for everything in my life.
- I must take responsibility for my actions.
- We are all doing the very best we can at any given moment, given the information we have at the time.
- I can only control myself.
- The important thing is to self-evaluate and consider what I contributed to any situation.
- We never know who we will connect with if we keep an open mind and have explicit goals.
- The Law of Attraction says that you will attract into your life whatever you focus on.
- Embrace aloneness.
- An overcomer can take any situation and turn it into something good.
- There are gifts, lessons, opportunities, and wisdom (GLOW) to discover in every one of our life-changing experiences.
- If we are continually looking in our rearview mirror, we don't know what is ahead.
- Figure out what you want and go for it.

Overcoming
Loneliness

"As you think, so you are." –Proverbs 23:7

*"Above all else, guard your heart, for everything you do
flows from it."* –Proverbs 4:23

The clock ticks. Otherwise, it is silent. It's a dreary, rainy day. I hear a motorcycle in the distance and look around from my seated position. Nothing has changed. The saucepan sits on the stove, crusted with dried spaghetti sauce from last night. The sink is full of my dirty dishes from the last two days. There is no one else in this house to make dirty dishes. No one else comes in and out of this house except for me. I can leave my clothes anywhere I want. I can leave my laundry in the dryer and not fold it for three days. I can keep the television on all night if I want to. I can leave the lights on in the kitchen or conserve energy and use candles. It doesn't matter because I am the only person in this house. The loneliness is overwhelming at times; the silence is deafening. I grabbed a book, but I'm not interested in reading today. I turn on the television, flipping through the hundreds of channels, but nothing grabs my attention. I go to the refrigerator—that will grab my attention. Eating, but eating alone. It's sad. What events led me to be here, in this lonely place I call home?

In chapter two of her book, *Secrets of Happy Couples: Loving Yourself, Your Partner, and Your Life*, "The Alone Stage," Kim Olver states, "We cannot be happy in any relationship unless we are happy being alone." She talks about the importance of loving yourself. Kim believes that the best way to experience happiness with your future partner is to first "embrace your alone time as a time for reflection, contemplation, and self-growth… introspectively assess whether or not you are the person you need to be to allow the person you seek to come into your life." After reading her book, I decided I no longer wanted to be lonely.

One day, I was in Macy's with my sister, and the sales associate in the cologne department followed us around, flaunting the latest product. I always thought it was silly to spend so much money on cologne—so expensive. But that day, I was intrigued. The woman greeted me with a smile, sat me down, and told me why this new men's cologne was so awesome. When she sprayed it on the paper strip, something sparked. I slowly wafted the dampened tester strip under my nose, shaking it as it passed. I felt a wave of excitement jolt through my body. Smelling it again, I knew that this was the cologne my next soulmate would wear when I found him.

My sister was less impressed with the scent than I was, but that's okay—it wasn't about her. It was about me knowing what I want and going out there and getting it. I bought that box of cologne all wrapped in cellophane. My sister could not believe it. She said, "You don't even have a boyfriend." I said, "I believe. I have hope. Someday, I will have a boyfriend, and when he proposes, I will give him this cologne". She thought I was crazy, but I decided I wanted to find a loving man and share my life with him. I brought that cologne home, and I put it on my dresser. I sat down and wrote a list of the criteria I desired if a man would come into my life. I wanted certain stipulations, and I wrote these down on a piece of paper. I folded that piece of paper and laid it right next to the cologne. The list contained non-negotiables such as being a non-smoker, no drugs, minimal drinking, and not being filled with anger. I also asked for no children under thirteen. More criteria included someone who loves to dance and loves physical contact. Those are the kinds of attributes I stored away in my mind.

I continued to heal myself. I regularly connected with a counselor, journaled, meditated, ate healthier, and even tried Yoga. Kim's book said we should celebrate the alone stage. I wasn't exactly sure what that meant, and I wasn't exactly sure if I could achieve that notion. Each day, I looked at that cologne and read the list of those twelve non-negotiables. I knew my God would provide exactly what I needed; I just needed to do the work.

If you're feeling lonely right now, becoming clear on what you want can be very helpful. I continued to read that list of criteria and knew I would never find my person if I continued to sit at home. I wanted to go dancing, but I believed that all dancing requires two people. I had become sullen and thought I would never go dancing again, even though "loves to dance" was one of the criteria on my list. I continued reading *Secrets of Happy Couples*. It said to get out and do the things you love to do. But I was scared to go out alone, to be alone in public, where people would stare at me. How could I dance alone as a woman with all those guys staring at me? I didn't want to dress too provocatively, but I also didn't want to be too matronly, so what could I wear?

I love going to the movies, but I stopped because I didn't have anyone to sit next to me and hold my hand. I realized that was silly, so I brought myself to a movie theater, sat there with my popcorn and drink, and watched the most beautiful movie alone. I was satisfied, and my mindset had changed—I could still do the things I love to do by myself. Finally, I was able to go dancing.

In times of loneliness, it's up to us to take that step out of the mindset that keeps us captive. You are the driver of your thoughts and actions, and taking control of these things can change how you feel. Metacognition is thinking about your thinking. If you stopped to think about your thinking, what are you thinking in this moment of loneliness? When you are feeling lonely, stop to consider what you are thinking about and what you are actually doing in those moments. When I'm alone in my house listening to that clock ticking, my heart sings because I know I am strong and courageous enough to get up, get out of that old thought pattern, and apply my new way of thinking. I changed something in my life. I had no idea of the chain effect that would occur by taking just one small step at a time, doing the next right thing. It's looking where you're going, not where you came from. This is how we move out of loneliness.

That cologne is no longer sitting unopened on my dresser, and I threw away that list of non-negotiables, because Aurelio, my husband, wears that cologne every time we go out dancing.

Do you think being alone is the same thing as being lonely? According to Vocabulary.com, alone is defined as being "isolated from others," and loneliness is "the state of being alone and feeling sad about it." So, if loneliness is a state of being and a feeling, can we change our feelings? The answer, of course, is "yes," but the bigger question is "how." As we've discussed before, we can gain control over our emotions by focusing on changing our thoughts and actions.

If you are trying to change your mindset, there are many resources: books, podcasts, and YouTube videos. Jon Wortmann is an executive and mental coach, minister speaker, and best-selling author of five books, and I had the opportunity to listen to him speak at my school one day. He made a statement that stuck with me: "Thinking and behaving is how we deal with our 'bio-self' and the feelings that arise from the complex process of being us." Our thoughts and actions have a huge impact and are critical to how we feel.

It is possible to be alone without feeling lonely. It is also possible to feel lonely in a large crowd of people. Once again, it is a state of mind. Whether I am with people or without people, loneliness can still occur. So, how do you take the next step when feeling lonely? The first thing to do is list everything you would be doing in a perfect world if you weren't lonely. The next step is to pick one thing off your list and set a time or a date by which that thing will be accomplished, whether it's the next hour, next day, or next month. Then, under that task, list the specific action steps you will need to take to achieve that task. These action steps should be very specific.

Here's an example: When I get home from work and no one is in my house, I feel lonely when it is time to eat dinner. I don't want to feel lonely. After labeling the feeling, I list all the things I would rather be doing: I would rather be sitting in a restaurant with company. I would rather be shopping. I would rather be walking on the beach. First, I choose which to conquer: I will conquer the goal of sitting in a restaurant with family members. Then, I set a goal and list specific steps that will help me achieve this goal. Within the next two weeks, I will schedule a time and a place to sit in a restaurant with one or two family members and enjoy one full meal together. This activity will then occur once a month. How can I ensure this happens? An accountability partner—a good friend you can count on to hold you accountable to reach your goals. You and your accountability partner decide how often you want to check in with each other. When you connect with your accountability partner, it is important that you are brutally honest with each other. Don't make any excuses. State the facts and discuss the next steps to reach your goal. If you and your accountability partner find that the task is too complicated, needs to be broken down, or wants to change the goal, you do that together.

During Kim Olver's podcast, *Life = Choices; Choices = Life* (episode 172), Patrick Jinks, a board-certified leadership coach, reiterates the importance of an accountability partner. He works with his accountability partner weekly using authentic self-expression and self-assessment. The accountability partner's job is to ask two questions and then listen:

1. Over the past week, when did you find yourself being the person you wanted to be?

2. Over the past week, when did you find yourself not being the person you wanted to be?

The partner should ask the questions and not judge the answer. There is no such thing as failure. Failure simply brings you closer to your goal. It merely means you need to rethink your next steps. You can apply this concept to anything you set your mind to. The key to making this work is to set attainable goals, be honest with yourself and your accountability partner, and maintain the seven caring habits when self-evaluating yourself, your course of action, and the outcomes. The seven caring habits—according to William Glasser, the developer of Choice Theory and Reality Therapy—are supporting, caring, encouraging, accepting, trusting, respecting, and negotiating differences. It is essential to use these habits consciously with ourselves.

If you embrace these connecting habits, especially with your relationship with yourself, you will find it a lot easier to reach your goals. So when you are experiencing the feeling of loneliness, if you consciously practice caring habits and accept, listen, support, encourage, trust, and respect yourself, you will be on your way to moving out of this feeling of loneliness.

The clock still ticks loudly. I am still alone, but I'm not lonely. I put a conscious effort into staving off loneliness when I am alone. Remember that you are entirely in control of every aspect of your being. Although this is hard to believe, it is true. You are powerful. You are in control and can achieve anything you put your mind to.

There was a time in my life when I put myself in a terrifying, lonely situation. In the Missions of Hope International office in Nairobi, Kenya, I have never felt more scared and lonely in my life. The director and the assistant director stared at me. The silence in the room was deafening. They could see and smell my fear. My mind was racing. A tear rolled down my cheek. What was I doing here? Why did I think I could return to Africa and accomplish this near-impossible task?

Just eighteen months prior, I had packed my bags, feeling anxious and excited, and headed to Africa on a two-week short-term mission trip with my church and fourteen other people. I had no idea this trip would change my life forever.

We had been meeting as a team and preparing for this mission trip for over six months. We watched videos about other teams on short-term mission trips, discussed our fears and needs, and journaled. We would be volunteering in Mathare Valley in Nairobi, Kenya; I was still determining the level of poverty I would be introduced to.

The trip was full of joy, love, sorrow, and pain. It was during that mission trip to Mathare Valley, among the top ten biggest slums in the world, that I experienced a life-changing chain of events. After a twenty-two-hour travel experience, we arrived safely on Friday afternoon and were escorted to our hotel.

Saturday was our orientation. We were verbally prepared for our introduction to the slum. We were told to leave all our belongings behind, stay close to our guides, not take pictures, and avoid eye contact. As we started our journey, the smell hit me like a wave of rotten food and sewage. It was almost unbearable. The eyes of the adults looked sullen and distant, but the kids came running up to us, grabbing our hands, hugging us, and shouting, "Muzungu, muzungu," which means someone with white skin in Swahili but can be used to refer to all foreigners. Seeing and smelling the slum made it real. The path was riddled with rocks and uneven ground. A dark river of sewage ran through the slum at every turn.

Children as young as two wandered around, playing with anything they could find. Hygiene was nonexistent. Many children did not have any shoes on. If they were lucky enough to have shoes, they were worn thin or were two sizes too big. Faces were strewn with blackened saliva, runny noses, and crusted snot. People stared in silence as we passed by. We silently finished our walk-through with emotions flaring. Our team quietly rode the bus to our hotel, where we could debrief. Tears flowed as we tried to process what we had seen and process our feelings on our first day here. My world had been rocked to no return.

Mathare is a collection of slums in Nairobi, Kenya, with a total population of 500,000 people, and the population of Mathare Valley alone is over 300,000 people, according to Wikipedia. At that time, the Missions of Hope International School System educated over 17,000 students in fourteen schools spread out across the Mathare Valley. Their mission is "to educate, empower, restore, and redeem disadvantaged children, families, and communities to transform lives through hope in Christ." Our mission for the trip to Kenya was to bring hope and joy to the people in the slums and work in the school system to assist the teachers in bringing more effective instruction. A typical classroom was filled with forty or fifty students sitting on wooden benches, four or five students to a bench. Each bench had a twelve-inch wooden plank attached to it. Most students had a composition book, and they often shared a pencil, which was no bigger than two inches long because it had been used by so many. Their primary instructional strategy was sheer memorization: The teacher speaks and the students repeat, over and over. The bathroom consisted of a hole in the ground with footprints on each side of the hole for better aiming. I tried very hard to use the bathroom only once per day. Bringing napkins from the hotel breakfast was imperative, as toilet paper was in short supply.

Lunch arrived in five-gallon buckets placed outside the classroom. Like a well-oiled machine, students lined up with their metal plates. Kale, beans, and yuca were slopped onto each plate. We watched in awe as students happily ate with their hands in their crowded classrooms. The students were simply happy to have food, as this might be the only meal they received all day. Being in the slums was extremely difficult, and I often fought back tears.

While working in the concrete classroom packed with fifty-two children, I looked around and realized I did not see any students with disabilities. As a special educator, I wanted to assist the teachers using my expertise as a leader in special education, but students with disabilities were not in school. As our short-term mission trip came to an end, through tearful goodbyes and joyful singing, we boarded our flight for the twenty-two-hour trip back to America

I definitely had a hard time jumping back into American society with all the materialistic items at our disposal. My heart was sad. For months, I prayed and prayed for balance. Work took over and normalcy evolved, but then the message arrived: "You will return to Nairobi, Kenya, and start special education programming for the Missions of Hope International school system." It was the craziest thing I've ever heard. Who in the world can drop everything and go live in another country for months on end? It would take time to implement new programming, and I was already working as a director of special education in Connecticut. I just let that thought simmer for months.

I firmly believe that all students with disabilities deserve the same education as any other student. However, I understand that different cultures feel differently about children with disabilities. Some people believe having a child who is disabled is a punishment from God. Those kids may be kept away from society so their parents can avoid facing the stigma. Those families, especially the children, feel isolated and alone.

One day, about six months after my return to America, that simmering thought bubbled up again. I suddenly felt the urge to talk to my pastor. I told him I couldn't get Kenya out of my mind. My heart was aching for the students with disabilities. I needed to go back and complete the mission, although I had yet to learn how to accomplish this task on my own. The pastor agreed to make some phone calls and start the planning process.

The plan to return to Kenya came alive. However, I did not account for the deep loneliness I would encounter. The following school year, I saved all my vacation days from work. I talked to my superintendent and explained the situation: If I kept my twenty vacation days from this year and twenty days from next year and squeezed them all into the summer months, I could go on the mission trip over the summer and still keep my job. My superintendent agreed and supported my mission. The local newspaper, the *Valley Independent Sentinel*, got involved and asked me to write a weekly column.

And off I went, just eighteen months after my first trip—but this time I was alone.

I took the twenty-two-hour trip on my own, weaving in and out of customs, immigration, and multiple airports, navigating the layovers and language barriers, until I landed once again in Nairobi. So there I was, exhausted, sitting in the office of Missions of Hope International School with the three Kenyans quietly awaiting my answer. I was scared and lonely. The question was, where do we begin?

Alone in my bed that night, I had never felt lonelier. What was I doing in a country alone, thinking I could accomplish a task so big? Who was I to think I could achieve this task? Whose big idea was it anyway? The negative self-talk always tries to niggle its way into my life—but I can overcome this negative self-talk. I must consciously realize what that voice tells me and then counteract it by changing my mindset and focusing on positive thoughts. I believe in the power of one: One person can make a difference. What we can accomplish when we put our minds to something is impressive. As I have been saying all along, you are an overcomer, just as I am an overcomer. With faith and love, anything is possible. We can change the world, one person at a time.

I defined my goal, explained the action steps, and determined which ones I could take within the next twenty-four hours. Sitting in front of the director the following day, with a clear head, I changed my posture, lifted my head, straightened my back, rolled my shoulders back, and laid out my action plan. Deep down, I was still trembling and unsure if it would work, but I knew I had to try. Someone believed in me; I pulled my strength from Him.

Over the next twelve weeks, I accomplished my goal. I had completed the development and implementation of a district-wide special education system. By the end of my time there, I had trained more than eighteen staff members on an introduction to disability. With translators beside me, I held forums in all fourteen school communities for the parents to understand more about disabilities. I leaned on the social workers in each community for support and protection. The stigma was real, and my presence angered some community members. After one month of educating the teachers and parents regarding disabilities, it was time to start assessing the children.

Once again, I was overwhelmed by the enormity of this task. With no supplies and no other experts, it seemed impossible. During conversations with summer interns and teachers from the Missions of Hope International School, we devised a plan for assessment. All the teachers from all the schools would pull the children they were concerned about out of their classes and bring them to a common area where we would assess them. I went to the library and started to gather books and materials that we could use to set up assessment stations. I found an abacus, flashcards, and books at various reading levels. Using the summer interns, we set up five tables. Each table had one intern and one Missions of Hope International School teacher I had explicitly trained regarding special education assessment. Summer interns were eager to assist in the process. The assessment day arrived, and so did the children. I was overwhelmed with emotion when I saw the lines of children waiting for their turn. At the end of the very long, exhausting day, we had identified over 153 students using the crude assessment system I had pulled together from the meager supplies in the library. The third month was spent rotating through the schools, helping teachers better understand how to assist the students we had identified.

For five weeks, I had been asking for a classroom to turn into a resource room. Space is at a premium in the Missions of Hope International school system. Under much duress, the resource room space was identified. The next step was to furnish it. In the slums, you don't just get out the catalog and order what you want. There is no mail delivery in the slums; Amazon is nonexistent. They make everything by hand. So, I was told to tell the carpenter what I wanted. I drew a picture of a kidney-shaped table and a cabinet with doors on paper and explained how tall they should be. I was told they would build this furniture, and I waited patiently. I wanted to see the finished product before I had to leave in four weeks. On my second-to-last day, I was called down to the room and could not believe my eyes. It was painted, the kidney table was perfect, and the cabinets were there. I started to cry. The Resource Room had come alive. Standing there, in that open space, as the social workers cried, I realized we really were going to change children's lives. I had never been prouder in my life.

There were many hurdles and challenges along the way. It certainly was not easy. I faced a week of darkness and deep loneliness during my stay. This darkness was almost impossible. I allowed the negative self-talk to take me over, but then I vowed to pull myself out of it.

For the time I was there, I became part of the Kenyan culture. They accepted me. I even drove their cars through the crowded streets in Nairobi. Driving on the left-hand side of the road was quite challenging. Despite the color of my skin, I fit in. Although I could never go anywhere alone, I became comfortable in their challenging environment with minimal sundries and supplies. But in the end, I had to come back home.

I left that August, a different person, and headed back to America. I had accomplished my task to assist the Missions of Hope International school system in understanding what a learning disability is and to ensure that all students deserve an education. I was sad because I had left the room empty, with no supplies for the teachers to work with. Although I left the room empty, the mission continued in October. Another group from our church filled that resource room with educational supplies. I returned to Mission of Health International in 2015 and made my fourth trip in 2023.

Over those eleven years, Missions of Hope International expanded that special education model program. They now serve 23,000 students in twenty-one schools, and every school has a resource room. Even though thousands of people live in that area, many still feel lonely. It is important to remember you do have a purpose in this world. You are a shining light for someone. Never underestimate the power of one. Our most significant growth comes out of the depths of our deepest worries and concerns. The power of one is real. You are more powerful than you ever imagined. When you learn to harness your inner strength, you will be unstoppable.

LESSONS LEARNED:

- Time goes by much more quickly when self-talk is positive and the outlook is clear.

- Choosing to love myself and understanding what I truly want is an action step.

- Get out and do what you love to do.

- It's up to us to take that step to get out of that negative mindset.

- You are the driver of your own behavior.

- Look in front of you, not behind you.

- Loneliness is a state of being and a feeling; we can change our feelings.

- You can be alone and not feel lonely.

- Actions require action steps. Action steps require planning.

- When you connect with your accountability partner, it is important that you are brutally honest with each other.

- There is no such thing as failure. Failure simply brings you closer to your goal.

- Every child deserves an education.

- Change your mindset by focusing on positive thoughts.

- Our most significant growth comes out of the depths of our deepest worries and concerns.

- The power of one is real.

- You are more powerful than you ever imagined.

OVERCOMING
Grief

He is gone

Addiction and death

Balance,

So delicate

wobble, fall, rise

over and over and over

Physically

Emotionally exhausting

Determined to conquer

Unrelenting, uncompromising

There is always a choice

Own it

Live with the consequences

Every moment

Unbury

Climb out of the depths of destruction

yet again

So close to death, yet still alive

Feeling only emptiness

Choices, every waking moment

I turn my eyes to the heavens

Shout out

Cry uncontrollably

I kneel down
I shake my fists and stomp my feet in anger
He is gone

No mother should outlive their child.

Here I am, three weeks after Ryan's passing, on an airplane headed to a consulting job. As I pass through the clouds, with the wing lights flashing in the fog, I'm looking for you, praying to see a sign; to feel a hug, a caress, a kiss on the cheek; or to hear a simple, "I love you, Mom." But it will never be again. I'm still staring out into the sky, waiting and wishing. Time goes by, and my heart still aches.

One year after my loss, I was headed to another consulting job in the same town. The memories don't fade; the pain constantly rips through me like a knife. As I walked into the lobby of the same hotel where I shared my horrible story with colleagues, I remember how my friends just stared at me in awe as I described what happened: My son was found dead in his bedroom with his feet still planted on the floor and his body bent over sideways. A piece of burnt foil was in his hand, a lighter on the floor, and some pills scattered on the table. There he was, still as can be, gone from this earth, and no longer in pain.

Ryan was such a happy-go-lucky child. His smile was contagious, and he spread joy wherever he went. He was calm and laid back, yet so aggressive on the drum set. But life is hard. At twenty-nine, he left us early. There is no rhyme or reason to it. The autopsy revealed an accidental overdose of fentanyl, Xanax, alcohol, ketamine, and cocaine barbiturates—a cocktail of drugs. That was in February. The prior October, I told his sisters to give him a call because I thought their brother might be depressed. They said, "No way, Mom, he's fine." When I asked Ryan, he answered, "Don't worry about me, Ma. I'm good." Then, we saw him again in November; he was training for his new job with Tesla. We all met for dinner, looking like one big happy family. Those are some of the last memories we have together.

Christmas arrived, and as usual, Ryan made the six-hour train ride to see us. The last gifts he gave us, now scattered around our home, offer bittersweet, gentle reminders of his presence. The day after Christmas, Ryan and I rode in silence to the train station, sharing some light conversation. I mostly remember his dog trying to jump in the front seat and Ryan telling her to get back. I unknowingly pulled into the wrong lane at the train station, completely ignoring the "do not enter" sign, and parked the car. At the realization, we laughed, as we did so many other times as he was growing up: We seemed to get ourselves in ridiculous predicaments, laughing all along the way.

He grabbed his backpack, and his dog followed as they meandered out of my car. Despite the laughter, he was not his bubbly self that morning. He had asked me to stop and buy some beer for the train ride, and I said, "No, it is eight in the morning, and I do not want you to miss your train." He looked worn out. I wished him well on his way. As usual, we exchanged a nice big bear hug. I said, "I love you, Ryan," and he said, "I love you more than you'll ever know, Ma."

It sounded out of place then, and now I know why. The Lord was preparing me for his departure, giving me that one last bear hug and loving conversation. I'm so grateful for that. I watched him walk away, backpack and all, dog running gently by his side. He never turned back around, just headed for the train station door. I never dreamed that would be the last time I saw him alive. It never crossed my mind that his soul would be taken so early. He was so convincing when he said, "Don't worry about me, Mom; I got this." So, I didn't worry about him. He was in recovery and doing great, or so we all thought. It's romantic to think God giveth and taketh, but that's not what happened in this situation. God would not steal a twenty-nine-year-old man. Ryan made a fatal error; he played a hand with the devil and lost.

I am always ready to see a glimpse of him, always prepared to feel a warm swish on my face and know it's him. I'm ready to know he is OK. I wait and settle in for now because I know I will never get another bear hug from him.

Grief is a feeling. Feelings come after our thoughts. We choose our actions, and our body reacts. It's complete. Have you ever heard the saying "change a thought, change a feeling" or "move a muscle, change a feeling"? It is a cliché saying, but it is true. How do you change your thoughts? First, we can focus on what we have, not what we don't have, and be committed to our goals, not our feelings. Then, we can overcome anything.

Overcoming is the core of my book—its mission is to lay the groundwork for you to see that you can overcome that obstacle, that thing that is weighing you down, the belittling self-talk that you're so used to vibrating in your mind, constantly telling you "no," the negative remarks others have made toward you lingering in your mind, those long days of not believing you can do it, the idea that no one believes in you and it will never get better. Does this sound familiar?

Do you have a relationship with yourself? The late William Glasser tells us that all problems are based on relationships. I will add that this includes the relationship you have with yourself. Are you a friend to yourself? Do you treat yourself kindly, with compassion? Are you empathetic to yourself? Do you love yourself? What kind of relationship do you have with yourself? This is one of the most important fundamental concepts and the first step in overcoming those obstacles. And are you in this for the long haul? I don't always like myself, but I do love myself. I don't always like what I say and do and my choices. I accept them because they are mine. However, we are human, and we all make mistakes.

The only way we learn is through our mistakes. I know you've heard that one hundred times, but it is essential to understand that it is truly the only way to move forward. In times of darkness, this is where we grow the most. This pain in the dark is so real and so hurtful at times, we think we're never going to get out. But that's when we start growing. There is always light.

Maya Angelou tells us fear and faith cannot live in the same space. And I love that thought, but I take it a little further. Am I going to choose faith or fear? Faith to work through, around, over, or under this obstacle or fear that I will never conquer? In trying times, I wonder how persistent I will be. How badly do I want to overcome this obstacle? Do I want to give up, or do I want to try a different direction? Why do I continually bang my head against the wall when it's not working? I may need to go over or under the wall, or I may need to sit quietly for a minute and gather my thoughts before I do anything. How persistent will I be in overcoming my grief?

The loss of my son was the most profound depth my mind, body, and soul have ever gone. No parent should lose their son. As I'm writing this, it's been over two years since his death. I think about him every day. For a few months, I was in deep despair. I was walking around like a zombie, staring out into space with no thoughts in my mind. People were offering their gracious and sincere apologies. Cards came to the house daily, and flowers were placed all over the house, but as time passed, the cards stopped coming, the flowers died, and the people stopped calling. It was just me, alone with myself and my thoughts. Life goes on for the living, but how do we take that next step in living?

There was a moment during my most profound grief, about three months after my son had passed. I was driving down the road. I wasn't thinking clearly. I had just been on the phone crying, talking to the life insurance company, trying to tie up all the loose ends that people forget about after a death occurs: the banking, the death certificate, the 401K plan with no beneficiary. Then there was selling the motorcycle, finding a home for the dog, and figuring out what to do with his beautiful drum sets— on and on and on.

I was at a red light. The traffic was speeding, and I watched car after car zoom by. How often had I sat at a red light and watched cars pass by hundreds of thousands of times? Where are my thoughts when I see these cars passing? That day, my thoughts were dark. For a split second and a split second only, I saw an eighteen-wheeler coming my way. It was as if time had stopped. The self-talk in my mind was muffled and very slow, as if it was in a tunnel with the mouth opening very wide and words coming very slowly, "What if I just drive out in front of this truck? Then I would not have to feel so bad." It was a fleeting moment, but it scared me. It's at that moment that I got to choose my next move. Will I drive out in front of that truck? Will it kill me? If it doesn't kill me, will I end up in the hospital? What if I survive, break my neck, and become paralyzed? What if I have internal bleeding and die a slow, painful death in the intensive care unit? I have two more children, my grandkids, my husband—I do have people in my life who love me. The truck sped by me in that split second; the red light continued to glare at me. These are the times I stop and change my thoughts so they align with the path I want to choose, leading me toward my goal. This season of my life was to grieve the loss of my son; my goal was to become mentally healthy again. Losing my life would not have helped me reach that goal. It would have been a selfish, self-serving, easy way out.

So, I joined a grief support group called Griefshare: From Mourning to Joy. I still do not find any joy in my son's death. I hope I can be joyful at some point, but right now, it still hurts. However, I have overcome that deep level of despair and moved back into the land of the living. My light has dimmed, but I am continually working to find the inner joy so that my light can shine brightly again. I am very aware that this takes lots of time and work. No one says it is easy.

I was unwilling to stay in that deep despair, physically walking around like a zombie, so I became very willful, obstinate in changing my thoughts and actions. In this grief, I suffered a mental breakdown. It was a very trying time for all involved. As strong as I thought I was, trying to push through the grief attacked my body at all levels. I knew it was essential to feel all my feelings and consciously process them. However, this can only occur when I am ready to process them, which is easier said than done. It takes time and conscious effort. How do we obstinately continue our course of recovery? This is the big question.

You may be struggling with an issue right now as you read this book, or you can think of a friend struggling with a problem. You may be grieving the loss of a job, marriage, or pet, or maybe the loss of a dream, innocence, or stability. We all suffer loss at some time in our lives. We all have the power within ourselves to persevere and persist through any obstacle. I genuinely believe that.

Did you know that we always get exactly what we want? Yes, we do. Henry Ford once said, "Whether you think you can or can't, you are right." Sometimes, we need to realize that we want things that will not bring us in the direction we want to go. When this occurs, you must stop and think about where you are headed. What road are you going down? What are your goals? Maybe your goal is to get through the next hour without eating chocolate cake or drinking a glass of wine. Maybe you want to read one chapter in a book or exercise twice a week. Whatever it is you're trying to attain, if you genuinely want to achieve it, you will persist and overcome any obstacle to achieving that goal. We all get stuck, though, and guess what? Sometimes, it feels good to be stuck. I like being stuck sometimes because then I get attention. Sometimes, I just lie around, sulking and watching TV; it feels good. Some people stay stuck throughout their whole lives. Are you stuck right now?

Back in high school, I was off-roading with my boyfriend and another couple, way out in the woods, up in New England. We had an F-150 truck, and my friends had a Bronco. The boys thought it would be fun, but I didn't realize it would involve so much mud! You can only imagine young teenage boys with their girlfriends in their cars, showing off for them.

I was hanging on for dear life as the boys decided to go through a big muddy puddle. The girls were screaming in fear, hanging onto the dashboard. The boys are simultaneously revving their engines and talking on the citizens' band, or CB, radio. Back then, there was a CB radio in everyone's truck. The chatter and engine were loud, and suddenly, we were in the middle of the mud, tires spinning. Deep and muddy water came seeping in the passenger door, leaking in at my feet. I was trying to be very brave, but I was so scared. It's funny how fear grabs you. I wonder what I was so frightened about. The only thing that could happen is getting stuck in the mud and needing someone to pull you out. However, I felt like I was going to die in that mud puddle, with the truck blowing up or getting sucked into a sinkhole. Our minds run in many directions, and when we allow fear to take hold, our thoughts become morbid. Remember, faith and fear cannot exist at the exact same moment. I wish I had known that back then, but I was young and naive. Then, as quickly as we went in, we were out.

The boys were delighted, hooting and hollering. This called for a dip of chewing tobacco to celebrate making it through the mud hole. A feeling of joy rushed through me. I could barely contain my excitement. But then the Bronco was genuinely stuck and needed help. We both got out and started walking toward the middle of the mud pond. As I got closer to the mud puddle, my feet sank deeper and deeper. Soon, the water was well over my knees. It had risen to the passenger door on both sides of the Bronco.

The boys were screaming, trying to figure out how they would get the truck out. The girls were trying to console each other. As I walked deeper into that murky puddle, the mud encompassed my boot, and the next step I took, my foot came right out. There I stood in the muddy puddle, up to my thighs in mud, with a bare foot hanging in the air. It was a predicament.

Have you ever tried to walk through mud and muck? It only works for a little while until you reach a breaking point. The key is what you do when you reach that breaking point. Do you start negative self-talk? *I never should have done this. I can't believe we're here. My mom's going to kill me. I'm in big trouble. This is the worst day of my life. What was I thinking?* Then, after that self-talk, I realized that it did not help me get my boot back. It did not help me get out of the situation in any fashion. How do I change my thinking? Tuchy Palmieri says, "Move a muscle, change a thought. Change a thought, and you can change your life." Our thoughts do control our lives. In that moment, I decided to take an action step rather than stay in the victim mode. I stuck my foot back in that mud and searched for my boot. I found it, and I started wiggling my foot. I started shaking, and amazingly, I freed my boot. That was the first hurdle. The next question was, do I turn around or continue? How persistent will I be in this quest to help my friend?

I wanted to think clearly. It takes a conscious effort to consider, especially in stressful times. My self-talk starts with calming myself down and thinking about what is in my control. What can I do in this situation? I had a clear goal in mind: I wanted to get home, and I was obstinate. I was stubbornly refusing to believe that we were stuck there forever. I was holding firm to my opinion and decided: *Let's figure out a way to get out of here.*

Can you think of a time when you were at one of your darkest moments? What were you thinking? What were you doing? Did you have a headache or stomachache? Were you crying or clenching your fists? Were you sleeping? How did you proceed? Do you still need to move? Maybe you're in the middle of your darkest moment now. Do you want to get out? Remember, we do gain some pleasure by staying in our dark moments. What benefits are you receiving when you remain in your dark moment? It is a fundamental question to answer. The next question to become clear on is, do you want to change the situation? We can be persistent and stay in that lifestyle, or we can be stubborn and move in a different direction. That urge only occurs when we feel the urge to change something.

My grief was overpowering my entire life, and I wanted something different. The grief comes in unexpected waves. However, it also allows for laser-sharp focus. It's like thinking through Jell-O and walking through molasses. I was thinking about Ryan's best friend, which led me to think about Ryan's best friend's wedding, which led me to consider that my son would never have a wedding, which led me to break down in tears.

I saw a picture on Facebook of one of Ryan's friends with their baby in their arms, which led me to consider Ryan having children—something he will never experience. He will never be a father or a husband. At Christmas this past year, one of Ryan's friends told me what Ryan said when he saw the friend's infant. Ryan said, "I can't wait to have kids." Once again, that moment led me to break down in tears. The grief starts in my stomach, and it works its way up to my chest. Once it reaches the heart, it bursts out of the throat—sometimes with a wail, sometimes with a gentle moan, but always with tears. On many Sundays in church, I wailed over the worship music, uncontrollably crying out to God, trying to figure it all out, until one day, I surrendered. The pain is too big to capture in words. However, I am confident it will calm down over time. The only way to calm it down is to remind myself of what I am in control of consciously. As impossible as it seems, I control my thoughts and actions. Grief takes time to heal. I knew I needed to allow my body to feel my emotions, but not wallow in them. I genuinely believe that, later, I will experience pure joy when I think of my son, just like the joy he spread when he lit up every room with his presence. There is a bigger plan; seeing it through the weeds is hard. I believe that Ryan led the life he was supposed to live—full of joy and love, touching so many other lives. I am sure his death will bring something else forth. I'm just not exactly sure what yet.

All will be well when my head matches my heart, but the disconnect still exists.

I will end with a quote from David Branon's book, *Beyond the Valley: Finding Hope in Life's Losses*: "It has become essential to grasp the difference between a life that is to be considered snuffed out suddenly without purpose or reason and a life that was taken from us under the caring, watchful eye of a God with a plan. It is important to remember that God does not make mistakes. God has his hand of control on my son's life."

Lessons Learned:

- The only way we learn is through our mistakes.

- I change my thoughts so they are more in line with the path I want to choose.

- Obstinately continue the course of recovery.

- We all have the power within ourselves to persevere and persist through any obstacle.

- Faith and fear cannot exist in the same moment.

- Self-talk starts with calming yourself down and thinking about what is in your control.

Overcoming an
Emotional Breakdown

"If you don't make time for your wellness, you will be forced to make time for your illness." –Joyce Sunada

Just six weeks after my son passed away, I tried working part-time, thinking it would help me work through the grief—but my body and mind were not ready for the stress. Our bodies and minds take in everything around us and process things at a cellular level. In his book *You Are the Placebo*, Joe Dispenza tells us that every thought we think, every emotion we feel, and every event we experience is under our control; we engineer our cells and control our destiny. Well, all this is well and good on a typical day. However, the brain has a difficult time functioning when experiencing deep grief. We must process grief in the body and mind. If it is not processed, a break might occur.

As a high-ranking educational leader in the public school system, my job was very visible. At our monthly meeting, my fellow administrators were seated around the table, anticipating the start of the session. I reached for one crucial piece of paper, and a realization broke me: I did not have it. It must have slipped my mind. Now what? Pretend like everything is okay. I looked up at the team, and I looked down at the table. Everyone was staring at me, and no one knew what to say. I got up and walked out of my office. My mind was broken, physically broken like rushing water through a dam. I stood outside my office in the waiting area, my administrative assistant gently peering at me with wondering eyes as my mind and body crumbled into a pile of mush. I wasn't sure what was happening. I could faintly hear my secretary saying, "Dr. Knapton, are you okay? What's wrong?"

Those words hit me like a brick. For once, I needed to be honest with myself. My thoughts screamed: *No, I'm not okay. My son just died—what do you think? It's not okay, nothing's okay. Will it ever be okay? There's a hole in my heart.* My knees wobbled, my whole body shaking as the tears flowed freely. What was happening? I could not believe I was this upset about a simple paper; I was breaking right before my own eyes. My secretary helped me sit down, out of the way of all others. Then, she proceeded to clear out the administrators from the meeting. No words were said. As hard as I tried, I could not stop the overwhelming distress at that moment.

My job was stressful and required mental clarity to produce results. I was incapable of mental clarity at that time; I realized I went back to work too soon. The profound loss needed to be processed—I needed to overcome that hurdle and climb that mountain before moving on to the next stage of life. I went home that day and went directly to bed.

We are strong and will overcome, but you must realize how many mountains you have before you and choose which ones you want to climb. We cannot climb all the hills at the same time. We need to choose our battles. And sometimes, we need a rest.

Parents realize this very quickly when they're raising a toddler. Two-year-olds want to be independent and do everything by themselves, but the adults understand toddlers aren't ready yet. However, toddlers require some freedom to explore independently for their development. This interaction can become a power struggle, with the parents saying "no" as the child ignores them. This exchange only worsens with time unless we understand its dynamics.

Do you think a parent can control a child? Let's process that for a moment. Can we control other people's feelings, other people's actions? No, we are only in control of ourselves. As parents, we teach our children things and influence them, but ultimately, the child chooses what they want to do. It's not a parent's job to control a child—only to keep the child safe. This interaction is a delicate balance. How can I attend to my own and my child's needs? We must pick our battles and choose what we want to stand firmly on, such as the non-negotiables. For instance, one of my non-negotiables with my grandchildren under the age of five is that they must hold an adult's hand when crossing the street. That is a non-negotiable. If the child does not want to hold my hand, I wait to cross the road until they are ready. Safety is non-negotiable, and it is a safety issue. Kids are smart. As my granddaughter got older, she asked if she could hold onto my shirt as we crossed the street. I said yes. We can't just let our kids run free, but if a two-year-old wants to tie their shoes alone, let them. Yes, as a parent, it will take you longer to get dressed and out of the house, and most likely, the child will get frustrated and may even break down and cry because they cannot tie their shoes. That is a skill they have yet to learn, but letting them attempt it anyway is a developmental stage they must go through as they become independent. These trials may bring the parent to their breaking point. When this occurs, step back, not forward. Don't lash out at the child. Can you think of a time when you hit your breaking point? What did you do? How did the situation get resolved?

When we hit our breaking point, it is essential to remember that we can only control ourselves. On that fateful day, my body sent me a message. As a leader, I needed to pick my battles. I did not realize how hard it would be to climb that mountain of grief and recovery. The toll it took on my body was a heavy lift.

I just kept thinking that it was just a piece of paper—one piece of paper I was missing for my meeting. In normal circumstances, I would have said, "Oh, hold on a minute." I would have found that paper in my desk, made copies, and brought it back to the discussion. It wasn't until months later, after I had given myself time to heal and process, that I figured out why I had broken down: I wanted to be perfect. I wanted people to see that I could return from a tragic event and be effective at my job. But that wasn't possible. I was trying to overcome too many things at the same time. I was trying to climb too many mountains at once when all I needed to do was lie down and rest. While we are all overcomers, we must be conscious of our emotional state and the deep, ever-changing trials our lives throw us. Sometimes we need to strategize how to go around or through the mountain instead of climbing over it.

Doctors and mental health professionals will try to ascertain the contributing factors to a mental health breakdown. They will ask questions, do a physical exam, and review records. High-stress jobs are a common risk factor for breakdowns. Some people are so embarrassed about their mental breakdown that they retreat into their homes. Depression, anxiety, and hopelessness can take over. Our minds can trick us, but we can fight back. And amazingly enough, we can fight back without the use of pharmaceuticals. Find a good cognitive behavioral therapist who understands Glasser's Choice Theory and Reality Therapy.

On that particular day, I drove myself home in a blank stupor. I felt like I couldn't even function. I kept telling myself, *Get home, get home, just get home.* When I got home, I went directly to bed, and I slept through the rest of that day. I got up, grabbed some food, and slept all night and the next day. When I awoke, I realized it was a turning point—the split second when I got to choose. I recall the famous quote often attributed to Viktor Frankl: "Between stimulus and response, there is a space. In that space is our power to choose our response. In our response lies our growth and freedom." In that moment, I chose between what was occurring around me and what I would do.

In other chapters of this book, I have described that we always have three choices: stay the course and do nothing, run and don't look back, or negotiate and consider alternatives to the current situation. I had to make a conscious decision: Am I going to stay in this mental state, or am I going to continue to overcome this mental state?

I decided to carry on with my grief recovery. I first had to admit that I had a mental break—no excuses, no blaming, no victim thinking. Just the facts: I broke, and now I get to heal. I started to define small, joyful events like sitting on my deck and listening to the birds, swinging in my hammock, reading a good book, relaxing, and reflecting on all the beautiful things in my life. We're in control of our actions, and I wanted to take action steps in the right direction. I could have run right to my doctor; they would have prescribed some Xanax, Ativan, or Vicodin. Undoubtedly, that would have helped me calm down. It would have kept me in a slumbering state of mind. My PCP did prescribe Xanax and Trazodone at the beginning of my grief. I think I took those medications for two days before deciding I did not want drugs.

Right after being prescribed these medications, I went to a William Glasser International Conference in Bogota, Colombia, with the National Institute of William Glasser. The keynote speaker was Peter Breggin, MD, a controversial psychiatrist and an expert in psychopharmacology. He has taught at many universities, has a private practice of psychiatry, and is the author of many scientific articles and books that discuss medication and Big Pharma. Dr. Breggin wholeheartedly believes we are over medicated as a society, and it truly is all about money. In his books, he advocates replacing psychiatrists' use of drugs and electroconvulsive therapy with psychotherapy, education, empathy, love, and broader human services. I remember hearing his keynote and thinking to myself, *Wow, he's right. We need compassion.*

As I have been saying over and over and over, relationships are key. It's all about relationships, not drugs, electroconvulsive therapy, and Big Pharma. Don't get me wrong, I am not saying that everyone should stop taking their medication. Dr. Breggin is correct. We depend on pills to make us better. We can improve ourselves, just as Dr. Dispenza and Dr. Glasser believed. One form of cognitive therapy is Reality Therapy. Dr. William Glasser developed it. He describes it in his book, *Choice Theory: A New Psychology of Personal Freedom.* When I woke up the next morning in Bogota after listening to Dr. Breggin speak, I realized I needed to figure out what I wanted. I was grieving the loss of my son, feeling down and lost, and I decided I didn't want to feel this way anymore—but that is a negative want. How could I turn that trial into a triumph? I wanted to feel joyful again, but I realized that was a huge step. Losing a child is devastating and could have long-lasting effects. It would take time, so I broke it down into smaller steps. If I want to feel joyful again, what must I think? Although I thought I might never feel joyful again, I understood I needed to be thinking that joy is attainable. So I started thinking that, as hard as it was to believe. I started thinking that joy could be in my life, even without prescriptions for anxiety, depression, and sleep disorders. I knew that medicine was only a bandage.

If I wanted to be joyful and thought it was possible, what did I have to do to make that happen? I enjoy sitting outside in my non-gravity chair, watching the clouds pass by, and listening to the birds. I enjoy reading good fiction books. I enjoy listening to classic vinyl music. I enjoy watching movies. These are all things that I could do for myself. After my mental break, I didn't do anything that first day. Just getting out of bed was a significant accomplishment. It is important to celebrate your achievements along the way, no matter how small. If I didn't want to continue on in this deep grief, I needed to continue thinking about what I could do to become joyful, and then I would have to get out of bed and do something. Two days after my mental break, I made it outside and sat on my porch for a few minutes. It can be challenging to decide to turn your trials into triumphs, and it often takes time.

Along my healing path, I suffered a lot of guilt. My thoughts were tricking me. I could not believe that I, of all people, had suffered an emotional collapse. As I continued to process my thoughts, I realized that it was my fault. Even though I could not control my body that day, I was in control of the events leading up to that day. It's about taking responsibility: I had gone back to work too soon and had suffered a mental breakdown. Although I refused to dwell on that, I needed to accept it. Believing that there was nothing I could do about it is the kind of thinking that leads to victimhood. We need to accept what is under our control and what is not. At first, I felt I needed to apologize to everybody in the room when I had that breakdown, but as I processed these thoughts of guilt and possible action steps, I realized it was none of their business.

I came across a helpful way to think about and visualize

responsibility. Grab a piece of paper and draw a small circle, then draw a larger circle around it. Now you have two spaces: an inner circle and an outer ring. In the outer ring, write down the things that you are not responsible for. This includes other people's actions, their opinions, their fears, their words, their mistakes, their beliefs, and the consequences of other people's actions. Next, in the inner circle, write down the things that truly are your responsibility—your own words, your behavior, your actions, your effort, your mistakes, your ideas, and the consequences that come from your choices. When you look at it laid out like this, it becomes much clearer. Most of what we worry about doesn't belong in our circle at all.

What people think of me is none of my business; it's what I think of myself that is my business. I should behave in the best way I know how to move closer to the person I want to be. If I want to be in a relationship with others, I will also consider their needs, but ultimately, what they think of me is none of my business. That is not a selfish concept—it is a fundamental concept and a very freeing thought. I will be the person I want to be with the hope that others will want to be around me, but if you don't like the person I am, it's truly none of my business. The only reason I would make someone's opinion of me my business is if I decided I wanted to be in a relationship with them. Therefore, I would work as a team to create a quality environment where both of us could meet our needs. I would notice how my behavior affected them and, depending on how meaningful that relationship is, I would decide if I wanted to change or not. I spent many years doing for others, looking good, and behaving how others wanted me to so everyone would like me. I always put on a smile to hide the tragedy I might be experiencing. These are strategies that can be used in certain circumstances for short periods, but living this way is unhealthy.

When I finally did go back to work weeks later, I still felt a strong urge to apologize to those administrators for my actions that day, but I talked myself out of that. I was experiencing a situation that I needed to deal with privately; no one else needed to know what was going on in my brain.

We never know what is happening with other people. Sometimes, our world breaks. However, those cracks in our world—the thin slivers of negative thoughts that can crowd your brain—are fantastic. These thoughts are telling you something. We need to listen for understanding, not just for what we want to hear. Those cracks that have taken over your thoughts, renting space in your head, are letting the light in—even if it is only a sliver of light and hope.

If you have experienced an emotional meltdown or you feel like you are building up to an emotional collapse, just remember, we all experience stressors. The important thing is deciding how you deal with them. Life is hard. There are many realities around us. We may feel challenged by them. However, you, in every single moment, get to choose how you will think and what you will do about the realities around you.

If you are experiencing any emotions around some challenges in your life, you can come out of it. You can overcome your thoughts, and you can change how you think and how you feel. It is possible; you just have to believe it is.

LESSONS LEARNED:

- Every thought we think, every emotion we feel, and every event we experience is under our control.

- We need to choose our battles.

- We are only in control of ourselves.

- As parents, we teach our children things and influence them, but in the end, the child chooses what they want to do.

- When we hit our breaking point, it is essential to remember that we can only control ourselves.

- We can fight depression, anxiety, and hopelessness without the use of pharmaceuticals.

- It can be challenging to decide to turn your trials into triumphs, and it often takes time.

- Behave in the best way you know how to move closer to the person you want to be.

- I will be the person I want to be with the hope that others will want to be around me, but if you don't like the person I am, it's truly none of my business.

- Your negative thoughts are telling you something. We need to listen for understanding, not just for what we want to hear.

- In every single moment, you get to choose how you are going to think and what you are going to do about the realities around you.

Overcoming
Dysfunctional Family Members

"Everyone you meet is fighting a battle you know nothing about.
Be kind. Always." –often attributed to Robin Williams

Growing up in my big family, I witnessed intense joy and deep sorrow. Of my siblings (Elizabeth, Alan, Christine, Ann, Susan, and Stanley Jr.), three of them have been at great odds with each other for years. I was always the one to try to mend the chasm, but it didn't always work so well.

Susan and I were Irish twins, just thirteen months apart. We were inseparable. Ten years ago, we watched the severe falling out between our older brother, Alan, and sister, Ann. In my infinite wisdom and continued understanding of the importance of relationships, I had woefully tried to assist Alan in mending this relationship with Ann over the years. They were estranged siblings in every way. The thing is, we never honestly know what others have gone through. Who am I to judge anyone for declining to be in a relationship with someone else, even if it is family?

All I knew was that I loved them both dearly. Their divide was painful, and I was sick of doing nothing. Their ruined relationship touched all our family events. We always had to be aware of the siblings who could not be in the same room together. I could never understand that concept, and over the years, I kept reminding them that they were brother and sister.

Always the middle child, I spent most of my life on the fence, calming people down. I never cared to take one side or another. Some of my siblings hated that, and some liked it. There were seven of us altogether.

Ultimately, I get to choose who I continue my relationships with. I want to feel loved. If a relationship isn't working for me, I can choose to leave it—but stepping away from a relationship with a family member is always more complex. The choice is always available, but guilt often takes over when making that break.

My brother was getting married late in life and had told Ann that she wasn't allowed to attend his wedding, but she took it upon herself to ride up north to my brother's house "to say hello" to Mom. Ann lived two hours away, so this was not a simple dropping in; this was a planned, deliberate, and willful act against Alan's wishes.

My mother and other family members were busily preparing for the wedding. When he had gotten word that Ann was on his property, I heard my brother before I saw him. We all froze in a state of high anxiety. The fear was palpable. I looked out the window to see Alan running down the driveway, arms flailing as he yelled profanities I had not heard in some time.

What a sight, I thought. *This was the brother I looked up to. This is my big brother. How could he be behaving like this?*

For some reason, maybe because I'm a middle child with an urge to mediate, I went outside and got between them. My fuming brother made no sign of stopping, his face as red as an apple. I pleaded with my sister to get back in her car for protection, and she eventually did, but she left her window down to continue her verbal vomit as she drove out of the driveway. His threats and her insults were zipping past my ears and crashing into the air. When she was finally gone, my brother turned to lash out at those of us left standing. He liked his alcohol and often became verbally abusive. His wedding day was no different.

Eventually, there came a realization for me as their sibling: it was never my business why this great divide was occurring, and I had no place trying to mend their relationship. I can only control myself and my own actions.

Relationships are like small rocks on the seashore. The waves crash over the rocks, the rocks wash up on the beach, and they roll back into the water. When the tide shrinks, the rocks sit on the sand—a period of tranquil calm as they bask in the sun. As the tide rises again, the rocks get touched by a light, gentle swish of water that eventually grows into waves crashing through. The calm is over, and the rocks are forced into an upheaval of torrential waters crashing upon them. The waves smooth the rocks over time, but the waves can also break them—it's a double-edged sword. The rock can become jagged and sharp, but the cycle continues, and over time, the water smooths the jagged edges once again. The cycle of dysfunction is precisely the same.

Think of a person in your life with whom you have experienced dysfunction and apply this scenario. I will use a clock face to demonstrate the cycle. You're engaging with this person, and it is high noon when this person demonstrates a behavior that knocks you off balance. Frustration and anger abound, and time ticks until three o'clock. Between three and six o'clock, you try desperately to control the other person into changing their behavior. Frustration heightens, and emotions are running high. Six o'clock marks the turning point when deciding whether to stay in this relationship. If you decide that you want to put energy into this relationship, then between six and nine o'clock is when you make amends. Sometimes, this is a two-way street, but it is often a one-way street in dysfunctional relationships, with one person making all the concessions to bring your emotional scales back into balance. Between nine o'clock and midnight is the period when you couldn't even imagine fighting with that person. You think to yourself, *Things are so good right now. How could I ever have a problem with this person?* Then the clock strikes midnight, and the cycle starts over—round and round and round you go. This cycle of dysfunction might occur multiple times in a day, once a week, or once every six months. Nevertheless, it is a cycle; you can choose if and when to stop it. But sometimes, people stay in dysfunctional relationships simply because the benefits outweigh the dysfunction.

I spent many years trying to control my siblings into behaving in ways that would make it easier to be around them. But again, I realized I cannot control or change anyone; I can only provide information. If the relationship is essential to me, I will let the other person know where I stand.

But sometimes, you might find you need to sever the relationship.

It is hard to describe precisely what happened to my relationship with my sisters Ann and Susan, but it came to a head as we sat, each of us over fifty years old, with my eighty-eight-year-old mother at a public restaurant.

The words sliced the air like a knife as Ann instigated Susan, and it was like a cork popping from a champagne bottle when Susan finally blew. She stood up and spewed profanities at everyone at the table before storming out of the restaurant. Mortified, the three of us sat in silence, staring in awe. Then Ann, who instigated the ordeal, asked us, "What did I do? How come she left?" There was no recognition that her behavior might have provoked Susan.

Susan was behaving in the best way she knew at that moment; the feelings that came over her and the thoughts that went through her mind produced the behavior of blowing up. While we can only control ourselves, we lose it sometimes—and that is a choice, believe it or not. After the seat was empty, I chose frustration and anger. These feelings are rare for me, but this time was different: I felt a need to take a side. So, I verbalized my perception of the situation. Ann became louder and louder, shouting profanities across the table, asking why I was protecting Susan. My mother sat in silence. All she ever wanted was for her children to get along. I was intrigued and hurt by how my mother behaved in this situation. I wondered how she could watch three of her adult children acting this way in a public venue and do absolutely nothing. As people stared and judged, my mother sat perfectly silent and still. The waitress eventually came over and asked us to leave.

If we stay present and conscious of our thoughts, we can be utterly content, whether we're basking in the sun, tumbling in the ocean waves, or crashing into other rocks. What I know for sure is that I can only control myself. I get to choose the relationships I want to be in. I get to decide whether I want to work on a relationship. If I want the relationship to prosper or grow, I might choose different behaviors, thoughts, and actions because I like the relationship to thrive. When I don't want the relationship to succeed, I demonstrate other thoughts, actions, and feelings, producing different behaviors. The cycle of dysfunction is similar to the cycle of abuse. However, you can choose personal freedom at any point during the cycle. It is challenging to deal with family members who you perceive to be exhibiting dysfunctional behaviors. We all behave in the best way possible at any given moment, so they might believe they are doing the right thing.

After that day, I consciously decided to sever my relationship with Ann. This was not the first time this kind of behavior had occurred, and I did not want to continue reaching out only to be swatted down again. I wanted to end the pain, the anger, and the dysfunctional cycle that continued to go round and round, year after year. The rock continues to be washed up on the shore, dragged unwillingly back into the ocean, washed up on the beach, and brought back into the sea. Does the rock ever get to settle down? When does that happen?

When offering my hand to try and connect with someone, they might take it to hold, grab it to yank me down, or turn away. However, as I reiterated time and time again, I cannot control anyone else's actions. I can't make anybody like me. I can't change the way they behave. So, I must decide if I will stay, try to make it work, or leave it alone.

I never formally told her I was severing our relationship. But after our mother passed away, Ann sent a letter to all the siblings, cutting us off from her life.

Sometimes, family members behave in a way that doesn't align with your way of being. Because it is a relative, we might let them treat us poorly, but remember, they can't make you feel bad; you choose to feel bad about their behavior. That is a tough pill to swallow.

All people behave the best way they know how, and some

people are not equipped with helpful coping mechanisms. If their behavior wasn't beneficial to them, they wouldn't behave that way. All behavior is purposeful: My sister is not mistreating me. She is merely doing the best she knows how, and I am choosing to feel inadequate based on her behavior.

Given that statement, I may not like how some people behave; that is my choice. When a person behaves in a certain way, and I choose to feel upset, it's empowering to know I can choose something different. I don't have to choose anger, frustration, or misery; I can choose freedom. If I know I am going to be in the presence of someone I tend to become upset with, I make an action plan ahead of time. I decide how I will behave when the other person exhibits unacceptable behavior. I put my hand in the air and calmly state, "I am unwilling to discuss this at this time." It has helped me in numerous situations.

Again, I know I can only control myself. So, if I find myself in a situation where someone is behaving in a way that is tipping my scales, I must first recognize that my scales are tipped. Then, I devise a behavior to bring my scales back in balance. Sometimes, I must prepare the behavior and keep it in my mind. For instance, one time at Thanksgiving dinner, one sibling started bad-mouthing other family members. In response, I chose the behavior that I had prepared. I put my hand in the air and said, "I'm unwilling to discuss this now." If the other person had continued, I would have left the room. It takes conscious effort to learn what behaviors tip my scale and choose different thoughts and actions to control my emotions. I only feel what I feel because of what I think and do. Nobody can *make* me angry or sad; I choose anger and sadness. With time and practice, I can train myself to choose something different. My counselor once told me, "You are in charge of your thoughts. No one can rent space in your head unless you let them." I love that.

If I feel people are treating me poorly or behaving in a way that doesn't align with the peace I want in my mind and soul, then it is my choice to decide how I want to handle it. The one caveat is that, when I choose how to think and act, my behavior should not be disrespectful toward the other person, should not be illegal, and should not infringe upon their needs as a person. Ultimately, it's up to you to choose which relationships to foster in your life. Just two years after my mom/s passing, Ann and I reconciled. The cycle is real, and you get to choose.

Lessons Learned:

- We never know what others have gone through.

- I can't control anyone but myself; all I can do is give and receive information.

- Each behavior we choose is the best we can come up with at that moment and benefits us in some way.

- I get to choose if I want to work on a relationship or not.

- They can't make you feel bad; you choose to feel bad about their behavior.

- I only feel what I feel because of what I think and do.

- Nobody can *make* me angry or sad; I choose how to feel.

Overcoming
Addiction

"Be alert and of sober mind. Your enemy, the devil, prowls around like a roaring lion looking for someone to devour." –1 Peter 5:8

The demon watches
Inching bait
Wrapping us tightly
In its grip of fate
 Feelings numbed
 With every sip
 The demon stays close
 Always on our lips
Slithering in
Not so kind
Hour by hour
Tricking the mind
 We think we got it
 We don't
 The mind stays hazy
 Take note
The poison constant
Coats the mind
Blinding the heart
Like no other kind
 Intoxicants thrive
 An arm's length away
 Choices, choices

> *Will they go or stay*
> *Hours upon hours*
> *Swept away*
> *Isolated*
> *in a stupor of haze*
> > *Memories wiped clear*
> > *What happened*
> > *The devil crafts*
> > *Did I do that*
> *The demon laughs*
> *He got his way*
> *The mind weeps*
> *We think we got it*
> *Not so; the demon creeps*

The dream that my children will someday get better has finally hit home. It is a dream, a want, an expectation, and I am not in control.

My children struggle with alcohol and drug addiction, and I often use alcohol as a crutch. That is the reality. We set ourselves up for failure when we want something we can't control. My son passed away, and my two girls struggled with addiction, rarely accessing any recovery support. My hard work as a parent can't make them want to change their behavior. My battered dream of raising productive, loving, empathetic, hard-working adults has been shattered, and I have finally accepted it as reality.

Julie is in her thirties now, and the pattern never changes—recovery, relapse, jail, pregnancy, over and over and over. The pain of my shattered dream, my hope for their happiness and peace, is more painful than the facts of reality.

Opioids stole my children: the giggles, the skipping feet in the hallway, the sound of crayons on paper, little feet hurrying to the bathroom in the middle of the night, the feeling of little hands rubbing my back and wrapping tightly around my neck to kiss me. Their demons are louder than my voice.

This roller coaster of emotions is painful, and pain is what first pulls us to the dark side—that place in your mind that convinces you to poison yourself so that you cannot feel the world. I went there for a while with alcohol, but I got a hold of myself before it ruined my life. My children weren't so lucky.

They left for college, happy-go-lucky children, and as time passed, I realized I had lost all of them to drugs and alcohol. The poisons took hold of them like a lion with a zebra in its mouth, thrashing around to live. But the damage was done, and the lion won. After the lion had his feed, the hyenas arrived. Soon after, vultures stripped the last pieces of meat from the carcass. That is what opioids did to my children.

Where did I go wrong? What could I have done differently? I carried guilt and shame for years. It was only through courageous therapy and support from family and friends that I realized I am not responsible for my adult children's behavior. That became my mantra, my saving grace: *I am not responsible for my adult children's behavior*. We all do the very best we can at any given time, and I did my very best as a mother to be a good role model for my children. I have finally learned to share my story without shame.

I was on an airplane traveling back from a consulting job, flipping through the movies, trying to decide what to watch. I never heard of the film *Beautiful Boy*. When I read the movie summary, I decided to watch it.

Have you ever sobbed on an airplane? I have.

That movie nailed it—my life story. Seeing it play out was more than I could handle. It was so strange to see, and the memories rushed in. I recalled how I used to drug test my children. Addicts are very good at getting around that, though. Many places sell fake urine; the challenge is keeping it at the right temperature for the test. Even though I understand we are all behaving in the best way we know how at any given moment, the lengths that people with an addiction will go to manipulate and disguise the truth so they can get their next high is incredible.

In the movie, there is a scene where a person with an addiction ransacks his mother's house, putting valuables he can sell in his backpack. The mother lets him stay in her house because she loves him so much and wants him to get better. It was the same for me.

Another scene shows a person with an addiction saving his overdosed girlfriend. Not everyone who overdoses dies. I know all my children have experienced this at least once, probably from both sides of the fence. My children have told me some of their own horror stories, and they are gut-wrenching. I once took a picture of my daughter in the emergency room. Julie had ingested bags of heroin so the police would not find any drugs on her. This is a picture I try to wipe out of my mind, but it creeps back in, and so does the doubt of sobriety.

There was a moment in the movie when the person with an addiction woke up in the hospital after overdosing. The doctor asked him what the problem was. The boy said, "I am an alcoholic and an addict." The doctor replied, "No. That is how you are dealing with the problem."

Continuing to blame the drugs for their behavior, I realized I was falling further and further away from the reality that my children chose to do that to themselves. Drugs and alcohol only numb the problem. People with an addiction must dig deep to uncover what the real problem is.

The late William Glasser would tell us that all problems are based on broken relationships, and this is also true with people with an addiction. I can tell you that it is incredibly challenging to maintain a loving relationship with a person with a substance use disorder. There came a time when I just had to turn my back.

I wonder if the people with an addiction watching the movie *Beautiful Boy* believed it captured their point of view.

At one point, the father says, "I can't save him, and I will not sacrifice my life for him." He had realized he wasn't present in his own life. I had gone through the same realization. For a period of time, I wasn't present at my job or for the other people in my life. But where do we find the strength to say "no" to our loved ones when they plead for help?

In the movie, the mother says, "He's going to die if we don't help him." The father responds, "He's going to die anyway, no matter what we do."

I always thought that if I helped my children get off the street, they would get better, but that only enables them to keep up their bad habits. My now-sober daughter once told me, "Mom, the best thing you ever did for me was tell me 'no.' You said you loved me with all your heart, but you would do it from afar." Addicts need to hit bottom themselves. I learned to love them best with my heart and soul, not monetary gifts, food, shelter, or clothing.

At the end of the movie, the parents go to an Alcoholics Anonymous family meeting, and they share the three Cs: I didn't cause it, I can't control it, and I can't cure it. I learned the three Cs from this movie, but I learned about a fourth C from an interview with an Alcoholics Anonymous member: I do not have to contribute to it.

How do I contribute to it? By doing for them what they can do for themselves, cushioning them from the effects and consequences of their bad choices, making excuses for them, and rescuing them. This allows the person with an addiction to avoid the natural consequences of their actions.

At the time, these words were not part of my vocabulary; they are now.

This quote from the movie sums up my feelings: "I lost my son [to drugs], but I never realized I was in mourning because even when he was here, he wasn't here. I always thought I had to stay strong." This great movie was based on the book *Beautiful Boy* by David Sheff. The boy the book is based on has been sober for eight years. Just for today, my story ends the same way with my girls, as they are both clean and sober now. It is too late for my son.

As a parent of adult children with severe drug and alcohol addiction, my mind often plays tricks on me. The pain of watching your child bounce back and forth between recovery and relapse is unbearable. Parents hope their values and morals stick with their children through adulthood. We want to think we can control our children, but that is untrue. Children behave when they value their relationship with their parents over their relationship with whatever is drawing them away. Unfortunately, the relationship an addict has with substances is stronger than the relationship they have with the people who care about them.

All problems can be traced back to relationships. As humans, we want to be in loving, connected environments. But sometimes, we can't be present in our own lives, so we form unhealthy bonds to things like drugs, alcohol, and gambling. The way out of unhealthy bonds is to form healthy bonds. Meanwhile, we put people who are not doing well in situations that make them feel even worse and then shame them for not recovering.

Beyond just individual recovery, we need to recover as a society. Something has gone wrong with us as a whole. We should build a society where we promote connections rather than disconnections. What if we did something different? In a Big Think article, "The 'opposite of addiction' theory: How community can drive recovery," I read about how the Netherlands decriminalized all drugs and funded programs that reconnected people with a substance use disorder to their communities. According to the article, as people living with addiction rediscovered their purpose, they became more connected and less addicted.

Disconnection is the biggest driver of addiction, and we live in an isolated society. While it is hard to love a person with an addiction, how can we build connections with them instead of shunning them? We can start by seeking to deepen the connection. Tell them, "I love you, no matter your state. I will come to sit with you. I will walk beside you. I believe in you."

The opposite of addiction is not sobriety; it is connection. In the throes of addiction, the only thing addicts care about is their next high—something that is especially hard to believe when there are babies involved. If there were no grandchildren in the picture, I would have left my daughter alone to live with her addiction.

The birth of your first grandchild is supposed to be a joyful occasion. My daughter, Julie, was five months pregnant when she was released from jail with an ankle bracelet on. I couldn't leave her on the streets, so she was released to me. The house rules were established, and the supervised, seemingly clean and sober months flew by. The birth was miraculous. My grandchild was named Xavier. I went home to rest, knowing mother and baby were safe and sound in the hospital. Upon my return, I noticed the nurse holding tight to Xavier with a look of disdain on her face. The blow hit hard. The supervising nurse pulled me aside and said, "We found cocaine in Xavier's system. The baby cannot leave the hospital until further notice." My knees buckled, and I almost fell. *My daughter would never endanger her baby like that,* I thought to myself. *The tests must be wrong.* It was a brutal reminder that addicts lie.

This innocent angel was born addicted to cocaine, going through withdrawal during the first days of his life.

The ensuing meeting with the Department of Child and Family Services (DCFS) was devastating and life changing. I never dreamed I would be bringing an infant into my house to care for while shunning my daughter. Time passed, and Julie was given more and more freedom with her child, and reunification was on the horizon. At eight months old, we split our time with Xavier: four days with me and three days with her. Julie always met me at her front door for the handoff, smiling and making small talk as I left. It was working out great. But addicts lie.

One day, Julie called me in tears, saying DCFS was sitting in her living room. The daycare made the call, and DCFS responded immediately.

It wasn't until I sat in her trashed apartment that I realized how bad things had spun out of control. There was an eviction notice lying on the table. The sink was full of dirty dishes, and the water had been turned off because no one had paid the water bill. My daughter's eight-inch high heels lay on the floor next to last night's dancing outfit.

The DCFS worker instructed me to take the child home. The next day, Julie voluntarily went to detox, then followed up with time in a rehabilitation center. During a DCFS investigation, which lasts forty-five days, it is up to the mother to follow DCFS's guidelines and work toward getting better. The courts are involved, so I had to stand before the judge and pledge that I was doing all the right things, only allowing my daughter to see the child for four hours per week. DCFS conducted surprise visits; I felt as though they were trying to catch us breaking the rules.

After the DCFS investigation, it was determined that the baby would live with me. Julie was allowed supervised visitation and was not to be alone with the baby.

My life was turned upside down. As a grandmother raising a child, life was hard; it's a challenging position to be put in. There are thousands of grandparents raising their grandchildren due to the addiction crisis in the U.S.

Only four years into my third marriage, my husband was willing to step up and go with me to a voluntary foster parenting class that was twenty-three hours long. We spent many weeknights studying to become licensed relative foster parents so we could move on to adoptive parents. We were doing everything right, but the third incident occurred on Friday morning.

I had this written down on Post-It notes that were pasted all over my house: *Addicts lie.*

It is very challenging to rebuild a trusting relationship after the trust has been broken so often on so many levels, but I believed my daughter was holding tight to her newfound sobriety. After a long conversation one evening and against my better judgment, I agreed to allow Julie's friend, Johnny, to take my car to drop the toddler off at daycare and turn in an application for work.

Hours after Johnny left, I received a call from a police department thirty miles away. He told me that my daughter, Julie, was driving twenty miles an hour down the middle of the street; she was arrested for a DUI and was sobering up in a jail cell. The policeman said a toddler, Xavier, was in the backseat without shoes or socks. It was the middle of winter, but the window was wide open. I asked the policeman where the child was, and he said a male friend had come to the scene, and they allowed him to take the child home.

I couldn't believe my ears. I was under DCFS watch. I was the guardian charged with keeping Xavier safe. Would I go to jail for this?

I had let Julie and Johnny borrow my car to run some errands that day, and they would come to pick me up at work. I had gotten a ride to work with a friend and was now stuck at work without my car, which had been impounded for the weekend.

This is life with an addict.

Thankfully, I found the child with Johnny. He had gone to the grocery store to buy a bottle, milk, diapers, and a blanket. He had kept Xavier safe all day.

I bummed a ride to the jail cell and picked up my daughter. She was hallucinating, babbling on about nonsense, and just kept asking where her cell phone was. Addicts love their cell phones—a connection to their next high. I asked her where Xavier was, and she said she did not know because Xavier was not in the car. I genuinely thank God her friend Johnny had kept the toddler safe all day.

I realized I needed to call DCFS and tell them what happened, but the police had already done that. When I arrived at my house, DCFS was already waiting in the driveway.

I was exhausted, disappointed, and scared of the outcome. Thankfully, after much arguing with DCFS, they agreed to let me keep my grandchild; Julie had to leave the house and not return—no more visitation rights.

When everyone left, I stood there crying in my living room, holding this innocent two-year-old child and wondering what the future would bring.

I vowed to keep Xavier safe as the cycle continued. After months of sobriety and DCFS involvement, Julie regained unsupervised visits with Xavier. He could go to her house for an overnight stay. So once a week, Xavier slept over at his mom's, but soon, I started to notice some troubling behaviors. Julie was losing her phone, losing money, and asking for a loan "just until the weekend." Addicts lie.

While I did not want to admit that I saw the signs of addiction creeping back into her life, I knew I had to protect Xavier. I contemplated the consequences of calling and not calling DCFS. Neither option presented a good outcome for me, but this was not about me—it was about three-year-old Xavier.

It was my day to pick up Xavier. Upon arriving at Julie's apartment, I found the door ajar, and it was eerily quiet. Julie was passed out on the couch, and a guy was passed out on the other couch. But where was Xavier? I searched the house and found him in the playpen. When my daughter stirred, her glassy eyes tried to meet mine, but her head was drooping as she nodded off. Suddenly snapping out of it, she said, "What are you doing here?" Tears swelled in my eyes. I didn't want it to be true, but I knew, and so did she. She jumped up and started tidying up the apartment. But it was too late; the damage was already done.

"I'm so tired," she said.

"Really? Why?" I asked. "What have you been doing? You don't have a job."

"Oh, well, you know, counseling and job hunting," she said. Those were lies, but she was always so convincing.

A few days before this, my husband wanted me to know he saw a car stop at our house when Julie was over for a visit. It was a white car with blackened windows and three people in it. So, I decided to ask, "Who was that the other day, coming to our house?"

Immediately, without any pause, she replied, "Oh, that was my neighbor coming to get his food stamps card. I bought food stamps from him."

It sounded like it could be true, so I decided to watch our house surveillance camera. I know her neighbor, but I watched someone I didn't recognize knock on the door while making a phone call. Julie, with Xander by her side, answered the door and let him in. He left two minutes later. As always, I confronted Julie after gathering my thoughts and facts. I showed her the video footage, but she stuck to her story. People with an addiction do; they hold on until death.

Julie had relapsed and was stuck in the throes of full-blown crack and heroin addiction again. She was lying through her teeth.

I grabbed my grandchild and left her apartment. Once home, I jumped on the Internet to start researching crack addiction. I learned that the high only lasts fifteen minutes, and crack is one of the hardest addictions to conquer.

As parents, we want to believe in our children. One of the first rules they learn is, "Don't lie," but then we proceed to lie to them for many years. *Mom, why are you and Daddy fighting? Why did Daddy throw that plate? Mommy, why are you crying?* I did my best to be a good role model, but being authentic and genuine is not easy amid chaos.

The child needed protection, so I called DCFS. It was the most challenging phone call, turning my daughter in to the authorities. The agency arrived quickly, questioning Julie, who was high. There we sat in my living room, with Xavier crying as Julie glared at me, venom spewing from her words. The DCFS worker was trying to make sense of it all.

Recovery is a lifelong process and a full-time job—not meant for the meek and only mastered by the most awesome.

Time went by, and the cycle continued—recovery, relapse, recovery, relapse. But what about the grandchild without a parent? His little arms were wrapped tightly around my neck, his head resting gently on my shoulder. He didn't have to say a word for me to know how he felt: abandoned, innocent, paying consequences for the actions of his parents. At just three years old, Xavier already understood the heartbreak of betrayal.

My guilt and rage went wild. *How could this be happening to me? Why did my children turn to drugs? What on Earth did I do wrong to cause this?*

My grandchild's father is a drug dealer. Just fourteen months ago, a drug dealer helped my son die of an overdose. *Should I snitch on the father? Will the police keep my number confidential, or will there be a hit out on me?* As my mind reeled, my husband stood firm—the rock—solid and helpful.

Finally, the day of the guardianship hearing arrived. Before the gavel pounds, the judge asks, "Are you ready to do this for eighteen years?" His words hung heavy in the air.

No, I am not ready to do this for the next eighteen years.

But I said "yes," trying to convince myself that it would be OK, thinking that I would find another solution, or maybe, just maybe, my daughter would beat the odds and recover. Most avenues to recovery involve a twelve-step program. Alcoholics Anonymous and Narcotics Anonymous are two of the most common. Celebrate Recovery is another program. The basis for these programs is believing in something greater than yourself, building healthy, supportive relationships, and doing for others as you would have them do unto you. These are also helpful for those of us who love people with an addiction. There is a saying, "Thank God for what you have and trust God for what you need." With an attitude of gratitude, I have been able to overcome the roller coaster of addiction in my family. I remind myself that I can influence them but cannot fix them, staying present while still protecting my heart.

I've loved to stay calm, listen attentively, and ask many questions. For example, Julie mentioned wanting to see her child more. So I asked her, "What must you do to see Xavier more?" She was silent, so I pressed on. "Do you miss your child enough to change what you are doing?"

Pain and problems are inevitable, but suffering is a choice.

One night, Xavier and I were on a little overnight vacation. The hotel room was dark and quiet. We had just finished reading our books and had said good night when I was given a sweet kiss on the cheek. Xavier wrapped his arms around my neck and said, "Happy Mother's Day, Nanny." In the darkness, I lay silent while tears streamed down my face. Prisons, institutions, and death had stolen so much from me. But, at that moment, I was in heaven.

Lessons Learned:

- I am not responsible for my adult children's behavior.

- Be brave enough to share your story without shame.

- The four C's: I didn't cause it, I can't control it, I can't cure it, and I won't contribute to it.

- A social community can beat the power of drugs.

- Disconnection is the biggest driver of addiction.

- Recovery is a lifelong process and a full-time job, not meant for the meek and only mastered by the most awesome.

- With an attitude of gratitude, I have been able to overcome the roller coaster of addiction in my family.

- I have the ability to influence my children, but I cannot fix them.

OVERCOMING
Painful Emotions

Anger, Guilt, Jealousy, Fear, Anxiety

"If an egg is broken by an outside force, life ends. If broken by an inside force, life begins. Great things always begin from the inside."
–often attributed to Jim Kwik

Emotions—they can bring the best of times and the worst of times. They can build us up and tear us down. What is really underneath our emotions? Where do our emotions come from? I know what it feels like to be joyful, fearful, angry, sad, or guilty, but can I control these emotions? I remember a time in my life when I was feeling very down. Life was not going my way. I remember dropping the kids off at school, returning home, and going to bed. I literally did nothing. This feeling lasted a few days. Dishes piled up in the sink. Scattered about the floor was dirty laundry. My hygiene was going downhill. The more my husband asked me what was wrong, the more I said nothing. I thought I might disappear. Would people forget about me? Then I remember thinking, *I don't like feeling this way, so what can I do to stop feeling this way?* The real key is to learn to understand our emotions so we can explore them and make informed decisions to respond to them or interrupt them. Our emotions are actually sending us a message. Learning how to read those messages is the next step.

Author Elena Aguilar wrote a book called *Onward: Cultivating*

Emotional Resilience in Educators. She talks about emotions in chapter two. She believes "emotions are a reaction that you have to an event. Something happens, your mind processes it, and your body responds. Then, you behave in response to your mind's interpretation and your body's response. Emotions are physiological, cognitive, and behavioral experiences." Aguilar describes six events in her cycle of emotions. The cool thing is that we can choose to intervene at any given point in the cycle and change our thoughts or actions. However, this takes practice. The six steps are the prompting event, our interpretation of the event, our physical response, our urge to act, taking action, and finally, the aftereffects.

William Glasser's Choice Theory explains emotions in much the same way. According to his book, *Choice Theory: A New Psychology of Personal Freedom*, real-world events occur, and we process the information through our value and knowledge filter. If we care about the information, we compare this information to our quality world—our idea of our own ideal reality. If it matches, we stay balanced and behave as we are used to behaving. If the information doesn't match our quality world, then we become imbalanced and dysregulated.

For example, here are some real-world promoting events: a flat tire and a screaming infant. Let's put these events through Aguilar's cycle of emotions in combination with the Glasser Choice Theory. First of all, step one is the prompting event. This is anything that happens outside of yourself, in the environment, or inside of you via a memory, a thought, or other emotions. In Choice Theory, it is called a real-world event. Step two is interpretation, when we try to make sense of the event. Aguilar explains that we put that event through filters of evaluation, understanding, beliefs, and assumptions. Glasser tells us that we filter the information through our valuing filter and our knowledge filter. Then, it lands in our perceived world. Either way, our mind is deciding if the event is important enough for us to continue processing it. For example, we look around to see why the child is screaming, or the tire might be flat on the car, and we discern whether we will continue acting.

Step three is the physical response. Our body usually has some physical response or physiology, like a fast heartbeat, clenching fists, or tears in our eyes. In Choice Theory, this is part of the Total Behavior concept of acting, thinking, feeling, and physiology. According to Choice Theory, it is all wrapped up in one concept and occurs simultaneously. Step four introduces the urge to act. Aguilar explains that this occurs alongside the physical response: You feel the urge to do something, which may or may not happen on impulse. You are now experiencing the feeling stage. Feelings might flood your mind, and you might be thinking of various ways you want to act. You might want to scream, throw the tire iron, or quietly fill the baby bottle with milk. Step five is action. We usually want to do an action (or behave, as stated in Choice Theory). Sometimes, we act on impulse, which can be very damaging.

When we stop, think, and process what is going on in our minds before acting, it is more likely that it will be the action step we want to take. In Choice Theory, we call this staying in balance or in more effective control. Using our examples, action steps might be to call AAA or comfort the crying child. Step six is the after effects. When all of that is done, we usually feel something else. We might feel relieved that help is on the way to fix our flat tire, or maybe the baby stopped crying because we found the bottle. Sometimes, our emotions trigger other emotions—like when you realize how late you will be for work and you feel angry. The cycle starts over again as you process these new emotions. Remember, you can intervene or choose to change anything in the cycle except the real world or prompting event. Life happens; we choose how to respond.

The critical part for us is learning how to identify and pinpoint our emotions. Once we identify and name them, we can act around them. Emotions are not good or bad, positive or negative—they simply send a message, and acknowledging that message is critically important. It is our response to the emotions that might be good or bad or right or wrong.

Erin Olivo, PhD, MPH, described eight core emotions from which all other emotions stem. In her book *Wise Minds*

Living: Master Your Emotions, Transform Your Life, she lists these standard labels for emotions: fear, anger, sadness, shame, jealousy, disgust, happiness, and love. Thinking about it, all our feelings can stem from these core emotions. Aguilar also tells us that emotions can turn into moods. If moods hang around long enough, they might become a diagnosis, such as depression or oppositional defiant disorder.

Let's do a little activity. Right now, I would like you just to be jealous. Be jealous. Jealousy is a feeling, and we're practicing how to just be. So, I'm asking you to be jealous. I can feel jealousy. But can you automatically feel jealous? No, our feelings are not automatic like our breathing or our heartbeat. Our feelings come to life after we think about something and start doing something a certain way. Then the feelings come, along with our physiology of stomach churns, clenched fists, thudding heartbeat, tears of joy, etc. We do not suddenly feel anything for no reason.

I'll give you an example. At the moment, I live a transitory life. I work in New Hampshire Monday through Friday and come home to Connecticut on Saturdays and Sundays. I love my husband with all my heart. We've been married for eight years now. This was a late-in-life marriage for both of us. We did not know this was where we would be when we walked down the aisle together, apart for five days, and together for two. The situation is neutral, but the way we feel about it and deal with it is our choice. I often think of military families and the time they spend apart. I recently watched an astronaut launch into space to live on the International Space Station for six months. She left her eight-year-old son and her husband on Earth. She wanted to do this. It fulfilled her needs. Although she would miss her husband and child dearly, she still pressed on. We all make choices.

Life is truly about relationships and the choices we make in those relationships. Remember, you also have a relationship with yourself. That is the most important relationship of all. In relationships, we try to balance our needs with those around us. It is not easy, but we can overcome the obstacles that stand before us. I have no concerns or worries about my relationship with my husband today. We both know and understand the situation. We both honor our time together and our time away from each other.

Worry and anxiety are two emotions that I feel are a waste of my time and energy. I realized that when I worry about something, it does not assist me in moving forward. It only holds me where I am or moves me backward. When I am worried, I try to acknowledge the feeling and look for answers. I see what is under my direct control. It is a waste of energy if I worry about something I cannot control, like the weather. I can, however, be mindful of the weather forecast and plan accordingly.

Since my husband and I only see each other on Saturdays and Sundays, we usually go to the movie theater or dance. It was a beautiful Saturday afternoon, and we hopped in his car to go to a movie together. Driving to the film, I noticed a can of raspberry lime seltzer water in his passenger door drink holder. I looked at the can. I jiggled it and felt it was half full. I know my husband does not drink raspberry lime seltzer water. A real-world, prompting event has occurred. I quickly recoiled my hand. I was deep in thought. *Who in the world would be sitting in the passenger seat of my husband's car?* I started to feel jealous. Within seconds, my mind spun in three directions, making up many things: *It was left over from a hitchhiker that he picked up. His middle school-aged godchild left it there when my husband picked him up from school. It was left there by his girlfriend. I haven't paid enough attention to my husband, who has gone astray. It's all my fault. How could I have let this happen?* My thoughts were racing.

I will call this level one. Our initial thoughts take us in many directions, and our emotions follow. If the thought is just an inkling, we could take it or leave it. Nothing happens. But, if we care about the person or situation, we decide to take it to level two: entertain the thought. Now what? A feeling attaches to the thought. Now, it is essential to sit back and realize what is happening. Things may go awry if I jump to conclusions and act impulsively. If I stay at level two long enough and continue to make things up that may or may not be true, I may jump to level three: absolute mayhem in my mind and body. My mind is racing, making it worse. *Who could be riding in his car with him? Does he ever have anybody in his car? He works alone. Were they coming back from the hotel? Was he in bed with someone else?*

Meanwhile, my husband is quietly driving down the road with no idea what is racing through my mind. All of this occurs within just seconds. My racing thoughts have become a giant snowball, growing bigger and bigger, until it is all consuming, while my partner quietly drives the car, unknowing what is happening in my mind.

We always have choices, and I am responsible for my behavior. If you look at the word responsible, you can see *response-able*, meaning we can choose a response. It is always our choice to respond. Hopefully, our response will help us feel more balanced. Sometimes, feeling more balanced means getting angry and taking action. Sometimes, it means stepping in, not stepping out, but other times it means shutting down. Every situation is different. The key is to label how you're feeling and understand why you are reacting the way you are. Own it. Be mindful that all behavior is purposeful, and when we behave, we are behaving in the best way we know how in that given moment with the information we have at the time.

So there I am, quietly riding in the car while my thoughts have ramped my emotions up to level three. What comes next is up to me. Can I take a breath and explore my emotions of jealousy and anger> What messages are they sending me? Are they based on truth or an assumption? Do I want to intervene or leave it alone? What road do I want to go down? Acting on impulse is never a good idea, such as asking, "Why would you have a can of soda in your car? You never have anybody riding with you in your car. Where did you go today anyway? I thought you were just headed to the house. Why were you so late getting home?" Stopping to analyze my thoughts keeps me out of trouble. The most important question I should be asking myself is this: *Is what I'm about to do or say going to bring me closer or further away from my goal?* Right now, my goal is to continue to have an amazing, loving relationship with my husband. If I allow the emotion of jealousy to take over, it will put a wedge in our relationship. Is there another way I could approach the situation?

What do I know to be true? There is a can of soda in my

husband's cup holder. That is the truth—nothing more, nothing less. The real-time or prompting event is not good or bad; it just is. But I felt fear. For me, fear keeps me frozen in my tracks. It stops me from progressing. When I fear something, I try to tell myself to "play it all the way out" and use the "five ands." For instance, I was afraid that my husband was having an affair. And: He must hate me. And: It is all my fault. And: We will never make it through this. And: I will be divorced again for the third time. And: What is my issue? Asking the "five ands" forces you to think about many different avenues of the situation and usually leads to absurd thinking that is exaggerated, untrue, and unhelpful. David Bayles and Ted Orland discuss fear in their book *Art and Fear: Observations on the Perils (and Rewards) of Artmaking*. They explain, "Fear is about yourself preventing you from doing your best work; fear is about your reception by others to prevent you from doing your work." Fear prevents us from moving forward, and we get stuck. If we are fearful, it is nearly impossible to make gains. Fear stems from something in our past that we fear in the future.

I experienced deep fear while doing mission work in Africa in the slums of the Mathare Valley in Nairobi, Kenya. We were waiting on a crowded corner to ride on a Matatu, a packed van much like a taxi. Most Americans would not be exposed to this deep level of slum life, but I was a resident for the last six weeks and would be there for six more weeks. My guide/translator was nearby but in training. I noticed someone walk by me with a watchful stare after he brushed my left shoulder. I was not carrying a purse and thought I had remembered to take off all my jewelry. What on Earth was he looking at? Fear gripped me as he approached again from the front, but I straightened my back and lifted my chin as a sign of confidence. He continued past me again, glaring at me. I stuck out like a sore thumb as the only white person brave enough to attempt to ride a Matatu with my guide. My thoughts were racing, and so was my heart, but I wanted to appear brave and courageous when, in reality, I was scared to death. My emotions were sending me a message. I was unsure what would happen if the locals got angry with me for interfering in their lifestyle. From behind, with his right hand, he grabbed my necklace, scratching my neck and yanking the gem with conviction. It happened quickly and swiftly, and he continued sauntering past me as he looked over his shoulder and grinned at my now tearful eyes. I felt so violated. I had been robbed, and my fears had come true. Fear is all-encompassing, and when I experience it, I try to weigh all aspects of my thinking.

Why did I fear this can of soda in my husband's cup holder so much? I can accept that it's there—done. Nothing more to say. Or, I have choices. I can gently and non-invasively ask a simple question. Or I can fly off the handle, sputtering obscenities and making crazy accusations. I can also gather more information about the situation to make an informed decision. We can always stop, analyze, and interpret our next move, though it's easier said than done. These painful emotions come all too often. When they occur, I ask myself if whether or not I want to feel this way. If the answer is yes, then I simply carry on. If the answer is no, then I make a conscious effort to intervene or interrupt the emotions that I am feeling. It doesn't always work.

I recall a day in the office. I was livid about a public statement someone had made regarding their perception of me. I said, "I am angry, and I am choosing to be angry right now," and then started spewing obscenities and flailing around like a crazy maniac. Then, I stopped and started to figure out what was in my control. I know it sounds wild. I know it's hard to believe that painful emotions are indeed under our control, but with practice, you, too, can understand and interpret your feelings.

Emotions are not negative emotions; they are simply emotions. The positive or negative spin comes from my values, judgments, knowledge base, background, and what I bring to the table when the situation occurs—my filters. You and I will not feel the same way about the same incident when it occurs. Things happen— not good, not bad, they just are. I put a good or bad spin on it based on what I want in life and what I believe should be the right way.

Let's think of an example. My daughter loves to buy scratch tickets. Even when she's broke, she will find a couple of dollars to go to the store and buy a scratch ticket. Then she sits at the kitchen table with her nickel and scratches the ticket. At this point, her emotions are running high. She is feeling excited and anticipating the joy of winning. Her mind was racing in a thousand different directions: How much money would she win, and when she won, what would she do with all this money? Gambling usually shoots your emotions up, and then you come crashing down when you don't get the outcome you wanted. On the other hand, let's consider that the same event elicits gravely different emotions in my mind. I'm wondering, *Why on Earth would I waste my hard-earned money on scratch tickets or even consider going to the casino?* I am not elated by the notion of gambling or scratch tickets, but my daughter buys them almost daily. The point is that our emotions are based on our values and knowledge base, what we believe is right and wrong, and what we think will keep us on the path to a quality life.

At the beginning of the chapter, I described multiple days when I felt very down. I wondered what I could do to stop feeling this way. I will tell you the first thing you can do is accept your feelings and label them. Remember, Dr. Olivo reminds us that we can categorize all our emotions into eight categories: fear, anger, sadness, shame, jealousy, disgust, happiness, and love. So label that emotion. Then, realize you are choosing this emotion. Choosing another emotion is one of the hardest things to do. But why would someone choose depressing—to feel so down?

Considering Glasser's Choice Theory that all behavior is purposeful, feeling down is the best way I can behave that day at that given moment, and there is a benefit for me. I can rest, get extra attention from my children and my husband. Maybe I will skip work and watch a lot of television. There are many, many benefits. We always behave in the best way we know how, and whether we see it or not, we benefit from our behavior. We will only change our thinking and feelings by deciding that we don't want to feel a certain way anymore.

Let's turn this around to a different feeling: guilt. Let's say I'm trying to lose weight. My sister asked me to go out to dinner, and while looking at the menu, I decided I wanted dessert: carrot cake with ice cream. I ordered it after eating a huge fried seafood platter, and I started to feel guilty, but then I asked myself, *What do I want more, the carrot cake or to lose weight?* I would then try to change my thoughts and start reminding myself that I don't have to feel guilty because I made a choice based on what I truly want. There are many other ways to feel, and I wanted to enjoy the carrot cake. I don't want to eat the carrot cake and feel guilty with every bite. After enjoying a fried seafood platter, I rationalized everything I could do to counter the effects of eating a huge piece of carrot cake. I could vow to exercise the next day. I could make sure I drink a lot of water. I could not have dessert for the next few weeks. There are options for me to play out rather than sit and feel guilty. I chose to change that emotion to joy, and I enjoyed every bite of that carrot cake because it met a need for me. At that moment, I wanted that carrot cake more than I wanted to eat healthily.

The first step is to identify the emotion, the second step is to realize that you benefit from this emotion, and the third step is to think about your thoughts. It's called metacognition. Think about what you're thinking; when you think about your thinking, you will be surprised how easy it is to change your thinking. Once you start thinking about what you're thinking, you're going to wonder what it would feel like if I changed my thoughts. When you consciously change your thoughts, you will also change your actions. You'd be surprised that your feelings change when you change your actions. So, we've labeled the emotion, decided that we want to change something, and now we've considered our thoughts. This understanding and analysis of our feelings can happen within seconds, or it can happen within minutes. Sometimes, when I'm in a deep emotion—like grieving the loss of a parent or grandparent, or feeling the continued emptiness of a divorce or a broken relationship—we must remember that our bodies and minds need time. I'm not saying that you can instantly take every emotion you're feeling and turn it into something else. We can start to believe that we can change painful emotions. We don't have to sit and wallow in anger, guilt, jealousy, fear, and anxiety—the option to take control is always there. I wouldn't say I like experiencing these painful emotions, so when they arise, I quickly start talking to myself, taking charge, and acting *response-able.*

We must pay attention to the bombardment of thoughts that come our way. The algorithms online shape us into the people they want us to become. You can shape the person you want to become. You can guide and curate your mind or consciousness to become one way or another.

I bet you are wondering how my car ride with my husband ended. While my jealousy was mounting, I started thinking about my thoughts, which is called metacognition. I wanted to take an action step that would assist me in trusting my husband and still get an answer to this out-of-the-ordinary event that has entrapped me. I was deciding what action step I wanted to take. If I did not address the situation, it would likely rot and boil out when we both least expected it. I tried to get answers now. I asked my husband, "Whose can of raspberry lime seltzer is this?" He just laughed at me without answering. Then I got even angrier and said, "Are you kidding me? You can't even answer the question?" He laughed again. When we arrived at the movie theater, he got out of the car and started to walk in. We often joke around with each other and use sarcasm as a mode of communication, so he thought I was joking and walked away as if nothing was happening.

Another prompting event has occurred, and my anger grew as I followed him into the movie theater. As he was chuckling, I had to make a conscious choice: How angry would I get? I labeled my emotions and wondered what was really true, what I was making up, and how important it was anyway.

I waited till we bought our tickets. Then I said, "You know I'm not trying to pry, but it really bothers me that there is a can in your passenger seat cup holder, and I can't explain why." At that point, he said, "Who did I go to lunch with today? Remember I told you?" And, of course, I remembered his friend had come up to help him with the electrical work, and they had gone off to Home Depot to buy parts. I had wound myself up over nothing, making all kinds of assumptions, and none were confirmed. I had forgotten that he had told me his friend would work with him today.

I am telling you this story to let you know that our emotions can bring the best and worst times. I often choose laughter and joy as emotions to live by: laugh, have fun, and feel pure joy. Are you stuck in painful emotions? Please know that you can control all your emotions, especially the painful ones. It is up to you to feel them, use the emotions as messengers, and take action.

I hope you have learned some strategies about how to overcome your emotions. Labeling them, understanding them, and then taking the steps you want or need to take is very helpful. It's a conscious choice to choose to be curious instead of angry. In these tumultuous times, with unprecedented sickness and social injustice occurring daily, it is very challenging to stay balanced emotionally. When I want to be angry, I label and act on that anger. That's OK. Please remember our emotions are helpful if we label them, understand them, and act on them appropriately. Do not let your story own you; you own your story.

LESSONS LEARNED:

- Life happens, and we choose how to respond.

- Our emotions are sending us a message, and learning how to read those messages is the next step. We are in control of our emotions when we identify and label them.

- The key is to label how you're feeling and understand why you are reacting the way you are.

- Determine whether what you're about to do or say brings you closer or further away from your goal.

- We can categorize all our emotions into fear, anger, sadness, shame, jealousy, disgust, happiness, and love.

- You can guide and curate your mind or consciousness to become one way or the other.

- It is up to you to feel your emotions, use them as messengers, and take action.

Overcoming
Negative Self-Talk

*"The biggest wall you have to climb is the one you build in your mind:
Never let your mind talk you out of your dreams, trick you into giving
up. Never let your mind become the greatest obstacle to success. If you
can put your mind on the right track, everything else will follow."*
–Roy T. Bennett

Could you imagine if all your thoughts were public—if everyone
could hear everything you were thinking? Our thoughts are so
powerful. They can be harmful or helpful as they shape the way
you feel about yourself. It is impossible to flourish while listening
to constant negative self-talk. Your Inner critic often drowns out
compliments and puts you down incessantly. When someone
tells you that you did an excellent job, that tiny voice in your
head might say, "Not really."

Thousands of thoughts flow steadily through our minds
daily. Our brain is a highly complex muscle. Information enters
through our senses, but our brain can only process these thoughts
and visions a few at a time.

For instance, have you driven down a road for the first time
and noticed a beautiful house? The next time you drive by, you
probably notice more about it: the landscaping, the flowers on
the porch, the color of the trim. Each time you see the same
scene, your mind processes more information. The mind makes
more room for more details as the initial information becomes
familiar. The same thing is true about our thoughts. When
our thoughts are familiar to us, such as negative self-talk, they

occupy our minds subconsciously, primarily when we dwell on them. Therefore, new, innovative, positive thoughts have no entry space.

Choice Theory helps us understand how our thoughts, actions, and feelings are connected. If I am thinking depressing thoughts, I am feeling depressed and vice versa. It is a package deal. However, we have more conscious control over our thoughts than our feelings. What thoughts are going through my mind, and what am I doing when I am feeling depressed? I'm probably feeling comfortable just lying in bed, sitting on the couch, watching TV, and moping around. I might even be complaining and thinking there is no way I can feel any better than I feel right now: depressed, tired, and worn out. That negative self-talk is constantly nagging us.

I experienced this nagging self-talk while trying to start writing this book. Over and over, my negative self-talk convinced me that I could never write this book. For years, I believed no one would want to hear what I said. I would tell myself there are plenty of other books on the shelves, and who would ever want to read about my measly life stories? But then the different voices would always chime in: *You have a lot to say, and plenty of people want to hear it.* It is funny, though, how the negative self-talk always outweighs the positive self-talk. Our brains are wired for negativity. That negative self-talk kept me from beginning my book for more than seven years. It wasn't until I finally decided that I genuinely had something unique to say that I eventually started writing this book.

As I developed my peer reviewer list, I wanted three reviewers to read each chapter—fifteen chapters, an introduction, and a conclusion. I did the math and decided there was no way I could find fifty-one people to review my chapters. I listened to the negative self-talk for weeks. I have yet to make progress on my writing. I could only think of two or three people. Then I asked myself, *Is this negative self-talk helping me get what I want—a list of peer reviewers?* I changed my mindset from "I can't accomplish this" to "I believe I can accomplish this." I started thinking that I could achieve it because whether I think I can or I think I can't,

I'm right. As soon as I gave up the negative self-talk and allowed myself the freedom to believe I could do it, I made a list of thirty-six, then thirty-eight, and finally, I had a list of forty-eight people. I was amazed.

We have direct control over our thoughts and actions, and they influence the way we feel. Negative self-talk keeps your mind and body in a hostile, ineffective cycle. When we are in tune with ourselves, our negative self-talk is relatively quiet because we have learned how to manage it. If you dive deep into Choice Theory, you will see that everyone's thoughts are just thoughts. When we start attaching emotions to our thoughts, that knocks us off balance, and we begin to feel those emotions that are ineffective. It is a cycle that most of us are way too familiar with.

For instance, when I wake up in the morning and am feeling good, I tell myself it's going to be a great day. I eat breakfast, make lunch, grab my bag and keys, and head out the door. I get to my car and notice my glove compartment is open, its contents strewn on the floor. After further investigation, I found that the emergency fund I had stashed in my glove box, a hundred-dollar bill, was gone. I immediately feel so violated. Now what? It is up to me to choose how I will behave.

We choose our behavior based on experience, values, morals, and knowledge. Clearly, we all understand that stealing is wrong. Having my car broken into meant someone came to my house, got in my car, and took my money. Those are the facts. The "good" or "bad" notion is my choice. Did I own anything in this scenario? The reality is just that, reality. We all perceive reality in our own way. We attach our feelings to the situation. Different people will exhibit wildly different behaviors in the same situation.

So, I'll give you two extremes for the thievery scenario. In the first scenario, I start right away with the painful self-talk: *I'm so stupid. I should have put cameras on the house to see what was happening. I can't believe I left my car unlocked last night. I'm so dumb.* I feel upset, frustrated, and useless—ineffective emotions tangled in these painful statements. I might start to get angry, raise my voice, and throw down my bag. I pace impatiently as I call the police, allowing my mind to spin uncontrollably into dysfunction—blaming others, criticizing the world for its poor values, and worrying about when this thief will come to my house the next time.

Let's take the same scenario and walk it through with a different mindset. I feel violated and frustrated that someone would come to my house and steal from me. The first thing I do is take a deep, calming breath. I need to take the next right step. What part of this did I play? Do I own any of this? I realize, yes, of course, I am responsible for some of this. Who leaves money in their glove compartment? Who leaves their car unlocked? I did. And now someone stole from me. I might say, "Well, I should have locked my car to protect the money in my glove box. The thief must have needed the money more than I did." This self-talk is very different from the negative self-talk. It's the same reality but with a different perspective, leading to a different outcome. Staying calm and keeping my thoughts as neutral as possible helps keep my actions neutral. This takes conscious effort until it is a learned behavior. You will remain angry until you are not angry. It is up to you. When you are no longer lost in the thoughts that lead you to anger, your newfound mindfulness can help you stop being angry.

Did you ever notice how unloving we are to ourselves at times? For thirty years, ever since I was in high school, I felt as though I was constantly thinking about my weight. I would try the latest diet with the best intentions. I would have the most positive self-talk for the first twenty-four hours, but when I would finally "cheat," the negative self-talk bombards me again: *There you go again, cheating on your diet; you'll never do it, you'll never get there, you can never follow a diet, you can never follow through, what's wrong with you? You are weak.* Then I would proceed to eat more than I ate before because I am not in effective control of my thoughts, actions, and emotions. It is not a very loving way to treat yourself; we wouldn't dream of saying these things to another person.

Can you think of a time within the last two weeks when you have experienced some negative or painful self-talk? Think back to the situation just before you started that negative self-talk.

What exactly was happening? That moment is the reality of the situation. Take yourself back to that situation and think about the moment, the moment of truth, the moment of choice, the moment when that reality hit you, and the moment when you chose negative self-talk. What different thoughts might have changed your actions? Would your behavior and feelings have changed, too? Can you reframe any negative statements and turn them into positive thoughts?

The thousands of thoughts crossing our minds daily are neither good nor bad; they are just thoughts. When we start labeling our thoughts evil or harmful or excellent and fabulous, we start taking action. However, I enjoy putting a positive spin on many of my thoughts because I begin behaving differently.

The last time I was single, I decided I was never getting married again. Single was a safe, comfortable place to be. Then, I met my future husband, and I started having feelings for him. I also had a lot of negative self-talk going on in my mind: *You have other things to do besides starting a relationship with a person in your late fifties. This relationship is going to be just like all the other relationships you've ever been in—dysfunctional.* I fought this negative self-talk daily. I did not have a picture of a healthy relationship, so how could I ever be in one? I had seen plenty of dysfunctional relationships over time, so as hard as I tried to talk myself out of this relationship, my heart was singing a different song. It was interesting to analyze my head and my heart. One day, I finally gave in and surrendered to this man. Taking a look at myself, I realized I am responsible for everything that happens in my life. I had already been divorced twice, and I couldn't just blame the ex-husbands for that. I needed to own some pieces of those damaged relationships.

When we sit back, take ownership of our lives, and realize that we are truly responsible for everything that happens to us, true transformation occurs. You become free to be the person you want to be. I was able to stop all the negative self-talk about relationships and let it be. The relationship blossomed into the most loving adult relationship I've ever had. Ten years later, we still feel the same way about each other.

My current husband is from Brazil, and we visited Brazil together. Of course, everybody spoke Portuguese, and I did not understand what they were saying. When I came home, I decided I was going to learn Portuguese. I purchased Rosetta Stone, and I started to "try" to learn Portuguese. There is no try; there is do or do not. When someone asked me about what I've been up to, I would say, "Oh, I'm trying to learn Portuguese." Then I realized no, I'm not. If it had been weeks since I last did a lesson, then I'm not trying. I am either learning Portuguese or I'm not. I could go off on a guilt trip using negative self-talk about always starting something and never finishing it, but the reality is simple: I am not studying Portuguese. If I want to attach some emotions to that, I can, but the truth is I'm not learning Portuguese today, at this time, at this point. If I were to start opening up my book and doing my lessons again, I would be studying Portuguese. We attach feelings to these statements because of our past experiences and also because of our goals, our wants, and our needs. If learning Portuguese is genuinely something I want to attain, it will outweigh all the other things I've been doing instead of doing my Portuguese, and I will learn it. It's my choice. Whether it's a good choice or a wrong choice, it's the best choice I can make at the time. Rather than beat myself up about it, I remember what is true.

I want you to do a little experiment. Get up and go about your day. Take a piece of paper and draw a line down the middle. On the right side, put the word "positive," and on the other side, write "negative." Carry this piece of paper with you during the day. When you have a thought, decide which column it belongs in. If you have labeled it positive, jot the thought down in the positive column. When you have a negative thought, jot the thought down in the negative column. Over time, you will realize that you are labeling these thoughts positive and negative, but thoughts are just thoughts. There is nothing positive or negative about them. Your labeling of positive and negative comes from your background, wants, needs, goals, and where you're headed. When things happen, you will label that a negative thought, which will not take you where you want to go. At the end of the day, see if you can learn anything from this list.

The bottom line is that thousands of thoughts are racing through our minds at any given second. We are paying attention to some of these thoughts, and some of them we are not. Keep your focus in the direction that you're going, whether you like it or not. If you're headed in a different direction than you want to be heading in, you should examine yourself. As painful as it sounds, you are responsible for almost everything that happens to you. (There are tragedies and bad people out there. Sometimes, you are in the wrong place at the wrong time.)

Whatever you're feeling right now is in your control. You can take hold of that steering wheel and drive your car in any direction you want. Choice Theory describes it like this: Your thoughts and actions are like the front wheels, and the back wheels are your emotions and physiology. You get to go wherever you want. Start paying attention to your thoughts and how you're behaving when these thoughts come across your mind.

A co-worker recently told me that I am the Valium for the office. At first I wondered what she meant by that, but now that I've thought about it, yes, I am Valium for the office. That is a huge compliment. That means I bring the calming factor to the people. When things get riled up, I stay neutral; I say what needs to be said. I don't get in the middle of everybody else's business. I just am. I understand that I am responsible for everything I think, do, and feel. That's a lot of responsibility, so I make conscious choices around others to act in specific ways. When everybody else is upset, jumping on the bandwagon to complain or argue about a particular situation, I can stay calm and take a minute to better problem-solve. It is a mindset, and it is a mindset that I have practiced over time. One of my colleagues shouted at me one day, "You need to remove those rose-colored glasses!" I said, "No, thank you."

I experienced many situations that taught me how to live this mindset. This doesn't mean that I never get upset, angry, or frustrated. It doesn't mean I never yell, scream, stomp my feet, growl, or shake my fists. All those things happen. What's cool about that is when I stomp my feet, I know I'm stomping my feet, and I might even say out loud, "I'm pretty pissed off right now!"

It might sound strange to label what's happening, but for me, it helps me remember that I am in control. If I want to be angry, I will certainly be angry. There are plenty of things in this world to be angry about. If we're not angry about some things happening in this world right now, then our eyes are not open.

However, I also try to remember I can only control myself. I cannot control anyone else or anyone else's actions. Therefore, I stay as calm as possible during any situation. However, if it is my time to advocate for something and fight, I'd better follow through. It is essential to stand up for what we believe in.

Negative self-talk only takes us down a horrible rabbit hole. If we're not careful, we will get stuck down there, and recovering from this harmful state of mind can be very challenging. I challenge you to start looking at your mindset and your self-talk. What are your voices saying to you?

Lessons Learned:

- Our thoughts are so powerful.

- The words you say to yourself shape the way you feel about yourself.

- Our brains are wired for negativity.

- I changed my mindset from "I can't accomplish this" to "I believe I can accomplish this."

- Whether I think I can or I think I can't, I'm right.

- Negative self-talk is a way to keep your mind and body in a hostile, ineffective cycle where you are not feeling in balance.

- When we feel in tune with ourselves, our negative self-talk is relatively quiet because we have learned how to manage it.

- We all perceive reality in our own way. We attach our feelings to the situation.

- Our painful self-talk only spins us into a downward spiral and keeps us spinning so we cannot make appropriate decisions.

- You can reframe negative statements and turn them into positive thoughts.

- I am responsible for everything that happens in my life.

- The thoughts are just thoughts. There is no positive or negative to them. Your labeling of positive and negative comes from your background, wants, needs, goals, and where you're headed.

- I understand that I am responsible for everything I think, do, and feel. That's a lot of responsibility, so I make conscious choices around others to act in specific ways.

- I can only control myself.

The New You

"I am not what I have done. I am what I have overcome."
–unknown author

We all need to find our way in this world. Life is hard, but it's only as complicated as you make it. How do we find the joy in the chaos? The remarkable thing is that we get to choose. There is no right or wrong path; there is just the path that you are on. When we start making judgments, that is when we veer off the path. Instead of wondering if what I'm doing is right or wrong, I choose to ask myself, "Am I feeling in or out of balance?"

Whatever path you're headed down, whatever course you've been on, or whatever way you think you're going to take are all part of what makes you who you are. Your perception of your past is your truth. Does your truth help you feel more in or out of balance? Is the direction you're heading in bringing you closer or further away from your goals?

Many of the concepts I talk about were informed by renowned author and speaker Kim Olver's latest book, *Mental Freedom: You Hold the Key*. If you want to dive deeper into the ideas I have touched on, her book would be an excellent resource. I am one of Kim's Certified Mental Freedom Coaches. I run online workshops to assist others in attaining more Mental Freedom.

As you know, I'm a middle child of seven children. After reading this book, you can see I have experienced many adventures. I'm not going to label them good or bad; they are what they are. My baby brother chose a different path than the rest of the family. I remember when he was eighteen years old, being inducted into the Church of Latter-day Saints. He had researched Mormon culture and wanted to live his life the

Mormon way. I went to his ceremony, and forty years later, he is still faithful to the Church of Jesus Christ of Latter-day Saints. He's been married to his wife for over thirty-five years, and they have four kids and ten grandchildren. I don't see him often because he lives across the country, but every Sunday, he sends all his siblings a "Sunday Thought." This keeps us connected, and we often add our opinions to the quotes. I particularly enjoyed a quote he shared by Elder Stanley G. Ellis:

"Hard makes us stronger, humbles us, and gives us a chance to prove ourselves... In the world of nature, hard is part of the circle of life. It is hard for a baby chick to hatch out of that tough eggshell. But when someone tries to make it easier, the chick does not develop the strength necessary to live. In a similar way, the struggle of a butterfly to escape the cocoon strengthens it for the life it will live. Through these examples, we see that hard is the constant! We all have challenges. The variable is our reaction to the hard."

This quote summarizes much of what I have discussed in this book. If you are going to overcome your obstacles, it will be hard. Complexity doesn't have to be hard. It's only hard if you make it hard. Fred Rogers once said, "Often, when you think you're at the end of something, you're at the beginning of something else." Are you at the beginning of something else? Embrace it. My brother did. I still love my little brother even though his lifestyle might differ from my own. We all need to find our way. Are you on a path that is helping you find your way? Don't allow one bad season to ruin the rest of your life. You can overcome.

Even after five years, I still experience triggers that throw my emotions into a whirlwind of despair. One day, when entering Guitar Center, I was unexpectedly overcome with deep sorrow. I froze, unable to step over the door jam. I quickly turned around as the tears poured out. Then, the wails of a mother who lost their child exploded out of me. Every Christmas, I shopped for my son at Guitar Center. He was a fantastic drummer. I stood outside the store, sobbing, using the tall cement pillar as a support. How do we turn our trials into triumphs? I allowed myself to feel the deep sorrow. I allowed myself to miss my son. I love and miss him terribly. As I continued to cry, people stared. No one said a word. None offered a hand. In that moment, that was precisely as it should be: I needed to be left alone to experience my emotions.

Life throws us challenges. It's up to us to decide how we will overcome these challenges. I decided I wanted to compose myself and enter the store, so that is precisely what I did. I'm not saying it was easy. Learning and growing are not always easy. I often meet people who know I lost my son. They say, "I don't know how you can keep it together. I don't know how you get out of bed each morning. I could never do it. You are stronger than I." Sometimes, I feel a bit guilty about my path, because society tells us that grieving mothers are supposed to stay grieving mothers— but it's not true. We can overcome our obstacles, even the death of a child.

I believe that we all possess an inner joy. Our internal drive and inner child help us shine if we allow ourselves to peel back the layers of grief and sorrow, trials and tribulations, successes and challenges, and strengths and weaknesses. We are all overcomers, one step at a time. Honestly, it is one step at a time, even if that step is moving to the couch after being in a deep depression in bed. The next step might be picking up the phone, calling your estranged sister, and telling her how much you love her. The next right action might be writing a letter to your father, who abused you. The next right step might be hugging yourself and letting yourself know you are enough, you are beautiful just as you are, and you have everything you need.

Although our past has shaped us, our present is what is real. If we take the opportunity to learn from our past and stay present in the moment, the picture will change. Taking the next right step, overcoming challenges, accepting trials and triumphs, and staying present are all strategies that will assist you as you look forward. Find joy in everything you do.

If you want something bad enough, you will do anything to get it. How badly do you want to overcome the obstacles in your way? What next step can you take to cross the obstacle before you? Do you genuinely believe that you can overcome trials and feel triumphant on the other side? I do.